Teaching Information Literacy Reframed

Teaching Information Literacy Reframed

50+ Framework-Based Exercises for Creating Information-Literate Learners

JOANNA M. BURKHARDT

Neal-Schuman

An imprint of the American Library Association

Chicago 2016

JOANNA M. BURKHARDT is collection management officer and director of the Narragansett Bay Campus and Providence Campus branch libraries of the University of Rhode Island. Her research has focused on information literacy and instruction, assessment, and collection development. She is lead author of *Teaching Information Literacy: 50 Standards-Based Exercises for College Students* and *Creating a Comprehensive Information Literacy Plan*. She has written numerous articles and made presentations about instruction and information literacy. She has reviewed books for *Library Journal* and *American Reference Books Annual* for more than thirty years.

ISBNs
978-0-8389-1397-0 (paper)
978-0-8389-1451-9 (PDF)
978-0-8389-1452-6 (ePub)
978-0-8389-1453-3 (Kindle)

Library of Congress Cataloging-in-Publication Data

Names: Burkhardt, Joanna M.
Title: Teaching information literacy reframed : 50+ framework-based exercises for creating information-literate learners / Joanna M. Burkhardt.
Description: Chicago : ALA Neal-Schuman, an imprint of the American Library Association, 2016. | Includes bibliographical references and index.
Identifiers: LCCN 2016004845| ISBN 9780838913970 (print : alk. paper) | ISBN 9780838914526 (epub) | ISBN 9780838914533 (kindle)
Subjects: LCSH: Information literacy—Study and teaching (Higher)
Classification: LCC ZA3075 .B87 2016 | DDC 028.7071/1—dc23 LC record available at https://lccn.loc.gov/2016004845

Book design by Kim Thornton in the Archer, Chaparral, and Avenir typefaces.

♾ This paper meets the requirements of ANSI/NISO Z39.48–1992 (Permanence of Paper).

Printed in the United States of America
20 19 18 17 16   5 4 3 2 1

*I dedicate this book to my husband, Michael, and
my daughter, Katie. Their unfailing encouragement,
support, and optimism make all things possible for me.*

Contents

Exercises

Acknowledgments

I WOULD LIKE TO ACKNOWLEDGE THE UNIVERSITY OF RHODE ISLAND LIBRARIES, WHERE much of my information literacy training and experience have taken place. I would also like to acknowledge all the other hardworking instruction librarians who have shared ideas and talked through concepts in information literacy with me over the years. Your insights have been invaluable.

Introduction

ONE FOCUS OF THIS BOOK IS ON UNDERSTANDING THE SIX THRESHOLD CONCEPTS outlined in the *Framework for Information Literacy for Higher Education* and on imagining how instructors might help students cross those thresholds. Another focus is on discovering how memory and transfer of learning apply to the teaching of information literacy. This book also offers some advice about how to design information literacy instruction that will be effective for both instructor and student.

The *Framework for Information Literacy for Higher Education (Framework)* is a new document. Although its creation took quite some time, its actual usefulness to the instruction of information literacy has yet to be tested. Because the *Framework* is conceptual in nature, there is very little practical information for instructors to apply in their classrooms. Because the document is a "framework," there are many gaps that must be filled in by individual instructors. The skin that will cover the *Framework* must be homegrown. The means by which this will happen is left to the individual institutions to determine. The *Framework* document urges librarians to work with faculty and administrators across their campuses to create a program of information literacy that will be incorporated into the curriculum in every subject on every level.

The *Framework* offers a description of the expert in information literacy but does not provide a roadmap to show how that person became an expert. The *Framework* describes what someone who is becoming information literate might think or do. It does not describe how to provide instruction for the beginner in information literacy, nor does it provide any guidance about instruction that will propel students over the six thresholds identified.

The six threshold concepts themselves are not easy to interpret. In some ways they mirror the learning objectives of the *Information Literacy Competency Standards for Higher Education (Standards)*. In striving to conceptualize the mechanics of the *Standards*, the clarity of language and the concrete nature of the examples in the *Standards* have been lost. The *Framework's* threshold concepts seem both hard to understand and hard to teach to.

This book offers a starting point for instructors of information literacy in understanding and teaching the six threshold concepts listed in the *Framework* document. The first chapter discusses the history of the development of the *Framework* document and briefly deconstructs the six threshold concepts. Then each threshold concept is unpacked in separate chapters along with exercises that can be incorporated in information literacy classes. The final chapter looks at learning, memory, and transfer of learning and provides some advice about how to design classroom exercises that will best help students master basic skills and concepts.

It is my hope that this book will help instructors create a local program of instruction for information literacy. Many of the exercises are designed for beginning students of information literacy. Others will be more useful for intermediate students. Some exercises can be used in the one-shot time frame whereas others are designed for longer class sessions and semester-long courses. Librarians have long been experts in adapting instruction ideas to fit their local need. I hope readers of this book will find some ideas they can work with to further the creation of information literate students.

chapter 1

Decoding the *Framework* for *Information Literacy*

THE **FRAMEWORK FOR INFORMATION LITERACY FOR HIGHER EDUCATION** is the product of a long process. In the late 1990s, the Association of College and Research Libraries (ACRL) responded to a need for students and instructors to move beyond demonstrating databases and learning which buttons to push. Students needed a more conceptual approach that would help them focus on the identification and retrieval of information they needed, rather than on which button to push in a specific database. ACRL created the *Information Literacy Competency Standards for Higher Education* as a guide for information literacy instruction:

> These standards were reviewed by the ACRL Standards Committee and approved by the Board of Directors of the Association of College and Research Libraries (ACRL) on January 18, 2000, at the Midwinter Meeting of the American Library Association in San Antonio, Texas. These standards were also endorsed by the American Association for Higher Education (October 1999) and the Council of Independent Colleges (February 2004).[1]

The purpose of the standards for information literacy in higher education was described as follows:

> Developing lifelong learners is central to the mission of higher education institutions. By ensuring that individuals have the intellectual abilities of reasoning and critical thinking, and by helping them con-

1

struct a framework for learning how to learn, colleges and universities provide the foundation for continued growth throughout their careers, as well as in their roles as informed citizens and members of communities. Information literacy is a key component of, and contributor to, lifelong learning. Information literacy competency extends learning beyond formal classroom settings and provides practice with self-directed investigations as individuals move into internships, first professional positions, and increasing responsibilities in all arenas of life. Because information literacy augments students' competency with evaluating, managing, and using information, it is now considered by several regional and discipline-based accreditation associations as a key outcome for college students.[2]

The *Information Literacy Competency Standards for Higher Education* document contains a definition of information literacy. The document briefly discusses the relationship between information literacy and technology, higher education, and pedagogy. It describes the goals of assessing competency in information literacy and the relevance of assessment of information literacy skills and concepts. The five standards and twenty-two performance indicators were used successfully during the next decade to explain information literacy to nonlibrarians, to help instructors plan lessons, and to implant a culture of assessment in higher education. Many institutions of higher education accepted the *Standards* and incorporated them in the curriculum across campus. Several of the national accrediting agencies added language concerning information literacy requirements to their standards.

In the 2010s ACRL appointed a task force to update the *Standards* to reflect changes, improvements, and the expansion of the concept of information literacy in higher education. Rather than simply updating the language, the task force changed directions and crafted a new document. This document, the *Framework for Information Literacy for Higher Education,* develops what the task force describes as "a richer, more complex set of core ideas" about information literacy.[3] The *Framework* is based on the notion of threshold concepts.

The threshold concept is best known from the literature of economics and the seminal work by Jan H. F. Meyer and Ray Land.[4] Threshold concepts are defined as

> core or foundational concepts that, once grasped by the learner, create new perspectives and ways of understanding a discipline or challenging knowledge domain. Such concepts produce transformation within the learner. Without them, the learner does not acquire expertise in that field of knowledge. Threshold concepts can be thought of as portals through which the learner must pass in order to develop new perspectives and wider understanding.[5]

Meyer and Land suggest five criteria that can be applied to identify threshold concepts. Threshold concepts are:

- Transformative—cause the learner to experience a shift in perspective
- Integrative—bring separate concepts together into a unified whole
- Irreversible—once grasped, cannot be un-grasped
- Troublesome—often counterintuitive; the place where students stumble or get stuck
- Bounded—may help define the boundaries of a particular discipline; are perhaps unique to the discipline

The ACRL task force decided to identify threshold concepts for information literacy and to use threshold concepts as a basis for creating a theoretical and philosophical framework for information literacy. Some of the threshold concepts reflect the research done by Townsend, Brunetti, and Hofer.[6] Several other threshold concepts emerged as input was received from information literacy practitioners and instructors. A draft of the *Framework* document was released on the ACRL website, and a call for feedback was sent out through various publications. Hearings were held online and at ALA Annual Conferences. As revisions appeared, the process was repeated. Meanwhile, the task force continued to meet and revise. Online forums occurred during the summer and fall of 2014. The final version of the *Framework for Information Literacy for Higher Education* was approved by ACRL in early 2015. (See the appendix for the full text of the *Framework*.)

Despite the task force's efforts to be inclusive and offer every opportunity for input, the number of people who actually responded was small. Those who responded were mostly librarians from two- and four-year colleges and universities. Little input was received from administrators, from schools of library science, or from students themselves. In addition, the debate about what threshold concepts are, how to identify them for information literacy, and the validity of the six specific threshold concepts that were identified or chosen continues. Still, the *Framework* appears to be a done deal because it has been accepted by the ACRL and has been put in place in the ACRL information literacy library of guiding documents.

Plans to sunset the older *Information Literacy Competency Standards for Higher Education* will leave instruction librarians with only the *Framework* on which to hang their curriculum. This situation could change in the future, but for now, the *Framework for Information Literacy for Higher Education* is the document that will guide instruction in information literacy.

The frames or threshold concepts identified in the *Framework* document are not self-explanatory. They are theoretical in nature and they don't offer much help to the instructor. In fact the document is quick to point out that "each library and its partners on campus will need to deploy these frames to best fit their own situation, including designing learning outcomes."[7] Although this approach gives absolute freedom to create instruction locally, it also puts the burden of creation on the local library instruction librarians—often people with very little time and very few resources to work with.

The *Framework* does not offer any hints or examples. It describes what an expert in information literacy does in the context of each threshold concept, but it does not suggest how the expert came by the expertise, nor how to introduce and/or develop those practices in the classroom. It describes knowledge practices—things that learners (nonexperts) do along the way to approach becoming an expert, but it does not give any information as to where they will learn or practice the listed abilities, or who will guide them. It lists dispositions—what learners often do to develop information literacy abilities—but it does not suggest the means by which such learners will develop the habits of mind that will eventually make learners into experts. All these considerations are left entirely to each institution to formulate individually. Ideally, of course, each institution will gather a task force that will produce a plan that will incorporate information literacy across the curriculum at increasing levels of complexity, with associated assessments throughout each student's college career, culminating in a capstone project that will show how well each graduate reflects the information literacy expert described in the *Framework* document. Most institutions will, in reality, be unable to even begin to reach this lofty goal.

For those few individuals who have reached an expert level of information literacy, the *Framework* document is unnecessary. According to the criteria for threshold concepts, those individuals who have crossed the thresholds to become "information literate" cannot unlearn their new way of viewing the subject. Having crossed the threshold, the information literate individual sees his subject matter differently and cannot return to his previous state. This makes it very difficult for those few to convey to the many information literacy beginners how to get across the thresholds identified. The experts must remember back to a time when they did not "know" and identify what they did in order to cross the threshold. Although the conceptual description of the threshold is present in the *Framework* document, the journey across that threshold is left to the imagination. We are given the destination, but we have to create our own map to get there.

The first appendix of the *Framework* gives suggestions for faculty and administrators about how to create a program that will provide information literacy instruction—although because it is a philosophical rather than a practical document, each institution will have to develop its own program for implementation.

> The *Framework* is a mechanism for guiding the development of information literacy programs within higher education institutions while also promoting discussion about the nature of key concepts in information in general education and disciplinary studies. The *Framework* encourages thinking about how librarians, faculty, and others can

address core or portal concepts and associated elements in the information field within the context of higher education. The *Framework* will help librarians contextualize and integrate information literacy for their institutions and will encourage a deeper understanding of what knowledge practices and dispositions an information literate student should develop. The *Framework* redefines the boundaries of what librarians teach and how they conceptualize the study of information within the curricula of higher education institutions.[8]

Appendix 1 of the *Framework* suggests a campus-wide approach to information literacy, much like the "writing across the curriculum" movement in higher education. For those lucky information literacy instructors who have the time, the support of administration and faculty, and the political, pedagogical, and personal power to effect change across a campus, this goal is easily accomplished. For vast numbers of librarians and institutions, the goal is extremely challenging. The *Framework* provides the *what* and the *why* but not the *how*. The *how* always contains the vital details about costs, personnel, and policy change. It is rare in most institutions of higher education to have the necessary personnel, funding, and time to create a how-to for planning a program of "information literacy across the curriculum," much less implement it. Appendix 2 of the *Framework* outlines the processes used to create the *Framework* document. As stated earlier, the processes used were open and tried to be inclusive. The time line shows a long trajectory to the final product. Appendix 3 of the *Framework* offers a bibliography of sources for further reading. None of these appendixes, however, provides any real, practical assistance to the librarian who must deliver information literacy instruction.

The good news is that everything we have previously created to help students learn to be information literate is probably still valid. The frames of the *Framework* are broad and indistinct. They overlap significantly. They are open to interpretation. Although they do not provide guidance in any practical sense of the word, neither do they limit. For librarians who are still teaching students only what buttons to push, it may be time to generalize from that lesson to a more global or conceptual message. Students certainly need to know how to use the tools that will be helpful to them in accomplishing their academic work. However, they also need to know how to acquire, select, and evaluate information beyond the academy. They need to be able to decide what information is valid, reliable, and accurate, whether their source of information is in a library database or on the open web. Perhaps it is time for the how-to instruction for individual databases to move to the realm of online tutorials, leaving more time to instruct students in the conceptual ideas concerning information and its uses. Even if a one-shot session is the only chance a librarian has to help students start their journey toward information literacy, the conceptual can be combined with the hands-on through the judicious use of technology and timing.

THE *FRAMEWORK* UNPACKED

The following six "frames" comprise the *Framework*:

1. Authority Is Constructed and Contextual
2. Information Creation as a Process
3. Information Has Value
4. Research as Inquiry
5. Scholarship as Conversation
6. Searching as Strategic Exploration

If we look at what each concept covers, it is fairly easy to see that what has gone before is still applicable. Researchers are not born. They learn to be researchers through instruction and practice. Students are not born information literate. They learn through instruction and practice. The instruction offered prior to the birth of the *Framework* still provides the pathway toward the expert status described. Instruction begins with basic skills that can be linked to more general concepts. As the student masters the basics, more conceptual material can be introduced. The *Framework* is conceptual in nature. Those concepts cannot be meaningful to beginners without some practical application and practice. The basic building blocks need to be learned before the concepts make any sense; therefore, much of the instruction designed to address the *Information Literacy Competency Standards* will apply to the threshold concepts in the *Framework for Information Literacy*. Looking at each of the threshold concepts individually may provide some clues about how to guide students toward the goal of information literacy.

Authority Is Constructed and Contextual

Information literate people consider *who* has created the information they are consuming. The relative expertise of the author should match the importance of getting an accurate and reliable answer. The more important it is to have accurate and reliable information, the more important it is to get the information from a recognized, credentialed authority. An authority in one field of inquiry may have different credentials than an authority in another field, so credentials that give someone authority can be different from one field to another.

Librarians have for many years recommended that beginning students use information generated by individuals whose credentials are relatively easy to find and assess. A PhD or an MD degree is a pretty good indication that an author has expertise in the field. We recommend to students that they seek out people with these kinds of easily discovered credentials until they have enough experience to evaluate other types of credentials on their own. More advanced students might be taught to match their information need with an authority whose credentials are not academic in nature, when that is appropriate. Students can be introduced to a variety of scenarios in which different kinds of authority would be acceptable or even desirable.

Information Creation as a Process

Different types of information are produced in different formats for different reasons. For each of these formats, different rules apply. The speed of publication, the depth of coverage, the size of the organization, the preferences of the editors or owners of the publishing machine, the formal or informal nature of the information, and the available technology all have an impact on the process of creating information in various formats. Because students tend to see all information sources as equal unless instructed otherwise, information literacy instructors recommend that beginning students use library-supplied sources selected by librarians, and we teach students how to use those sources. This strategy provides a safe starting place for students while they are learning how to select their own sources. As students learn about different types of sources, they should also learn about how the format of those sources affects the content.

Fortunately, it is still relevant to point out to students the differences between a newspaper story and a scholarly journal article. It is still relevant to provide a checklist of what to look for in online publications to help identify different types of information. It is still relevant to link the type of publication to its ability to supply the necessary amount of information to answer a specific information need. It is, arguably, even more important now than ever before to teach students to think about what type of source should be selected to inform a specific information need. The type of information needed may necessitate the use of a specific format for that information.

Information Has Value

Information is property and, therefore, it has value. In many countries that value is protected by copyright and acknowledged through citation. Information is often gathered and held by organizations. Some organizations institute a pay wall that limits access to the information (if you can't afford to pay for the information, you can't get it). This restriction gives the information monetary value. The ethical and practical considerations of limiting access to information have in turn resulted in a movement toward open access and other means of making information freely available.

Information literacy instructors have long taught the intricacies of citation and the evils of plagiarism. There is no reason to discontinue this practice. The ethical use of information has been an essential part of what any student should know. Teaching students about pay walls and access may, at this moment, be relevant. In the not too distant future, the distinction between business models and the effect of those business models on the information produced could become irrelevant. The idea that information is a commodity that is owned by someone is not difficult to demonstrate, whether ownership is linked to access or not. Teaching respect for the ownership of information is a long-standing practice in information literacy. Ethical use of information is a concept that students struggle to understand. Instruction in the value of information may help make the rules about using information more understandable. Students should understand the value of information about themselves. Some people share personal information readily and freely. Others may be less accommodating in sharing personal identifiers. We need to teach students about how third parties collect personal information and about the uses of that personal information by third parties. Students need to understand that privacy can be compromised in numerous ways.

Research as Inquiry

Inquiry involves a process of asking and re-asking questions, identifying new questions, and seeking unanswered questions. To investigate topics one may need to use more than one source and more than one type of source. Information must be organized and considered for applicability to the problem. Researchers must consider the scope of their questions and gather information accordingly. Ideas must be synthesized, and conclusions must be drawn.

This inquiry process is and has always been what research is all about. Librarians and classroom faculty have instructed researchers about this process. They were doing so long before the process was called information literacy. In fact, in the not too distant past, each discipline at most universities had a course called Research Methods in which techniques and processes for research were taught. When this body of teaching moved to the library, it became part of the information literacy continuum. Students need to learn that multiple sources of information exist. As beginners they need to learn how to use one or two before they can begin to consider using multiple sources to address a question. Most students begin and end their research with Google, often because they are not aware that other sources exist. One basic idea that can be conveyed in this part of the *Framework* is that multiple sources of information exist. Although most librarians don't have the time to teach students about every possible source of information, they can certainly demonstrate to students that a wide variety of sources is available.

Scholarship as Conversation

Scholarship develops through the interaction of scholars, be it in person, through technology, or by publication. The conversation develops in fits and starts and continues over the long term. Scholars talk to each other and, in doing so, move knowledge and understanding forward. Much of this conversation is invisible to those outside the academy, as it takes place in offices, hallways, and coffee shops and between meetings at conferences. In the past, nonexperts were not expected to contribute to the conversation, but they could benefit by studying the published results of the conversation.

Information literacy instruction in the past has addressed the published portion of the scholarly conversation. Instruction in creating and using bibliographies, citation indexes, and impact ratings speaks to the conversation of scholarship. What is different about the modern scholarly conversation are the new avenues that allow everyone who has an interest to be part of it. Students in the Internet age may participate in scholarly conversations by means of online forums, blogs, interest groups, and so on.

They may publish their own thoughts inside and outside the academy as well. Information literacy instruction can show students how and where this participation happens.

Searching as Strategic Exploration

The search for information usually begins with a general topic. As one learns more about that topic, it is possible to narrow and refine the topic. As one learns still more, it is possible and sometimes necessary to revise search strategies and to use different sources. This process requires the researcher to be flexible, to use critical thinking skills, and to keep an open mind.

Information literacy has long included brainstorming as a means of solidifying and narrowing topics of interest. Information literacy instruction may teach students how to move from a broad topic to a narrow question. Instruction helps students discover possible sources of information. It assists students by informing them about options for searching using keywords, Boolean operators, proximity limiters, and so on. By introducing something as simple as keyword synonyms, information literacy instruction teaches flexibility. In teaching the evaluation of sources, information literacy promotes critical thinking skills. Strategic exploration has long been a practice for information literacy instructors.

THE *FRAMEWORK* IN ACTION

Much of what has been devised to teach concepts and skills in information literacy applies whether the reference point is the *Information Literacy Competency Standards* or the *Framework for Information Literacy*. The student has to begin somewhere and usually requires guidance and practice. In some cases, this beginning practice is all the instruction the information literacy librarian has time and opportunity to provide. The trick is to incorporate into the basic instruction a persistent question or a habit of mind that will guide the beginning student to the next level on the journey toward expertise. If students learn to habitually ask *why* as beginners, that habit will continue as they reach higher levels of expertise and will help make them more strategic in their searching.

The *Framework for Information Literacy* provides a conceptual structure that requires information literacy instructors to fill in the empty spaces. The document offers a lofty view of what an expert in information literacy looks like. It describes six threshold concepts about which targeted instruction is needed to guide students to the next level of understanding. Information literacy instructors are urged to create this instruction based on their local needs. Because one cannot cross any academic threshold without some basic understanding of how to find good information, the many, many lessons created for information literacy instruction are likely to remain useful as a starting point.

With or without the conceptual *Framework for Information Literacy*, students need to learn how to deal with the ocean of information that surrounds them. In order to be successful workers, parents, and citizens of the world, they must learn how to obtain the information they need from the vastness of the information that is available. They need to be persistent in the search for information. They must learn to evaluate what they find by asking questions and testing the answers they choose. They must learn to question authority and search for bias. Students must learn to be aware of the means by which information is produced and how the means affect the content. They need to be savvy consumers and producers of information of all kinds. Students must understand that they can and should be part of the conversation.

The remainder of this book provides some ideas about how to make students aware of what information is, what forms it comes in, who creates it, and how it can and should be used. The exercises were created with the *Framework* threshold concepts in mind, beginning with basic ideas and working toward more complex concepts. The exercises are designed to create a trajectory that will move students toward each of the named thresholds and perhaps help them across those thresholds. The exercises provide a starting point for instruction in information literacy and will, it is hoped, provoke additional ideas and approaches. As with any other endeavor, it helps to have a place to start and some ideas to start with.

NOTES

1. Association of College and Research Libraries, *Information Literacy Competency Standards for Higher Education* (Chicago: American Library Association, 2000), www.ala.org/acrl/standards/informationliteracycompetency.

2. Association of College and Research Libraries, "Information Literacy and Higher Education," *Information Literacy Competency Standards for Higher Education* (Chicago: American Library Association, 2000), www.ala.org/acrl/standards/informationliteracy competency#ilhed.

3. Association of College and Research Libraries, *Framework for Information Literacy for Higher Education* (Chicago: American Library Association, 2015), 1, www.ala.org/acrl/standards/ilframework.

4. J. H. F. Meyer and M. Shanahan, "The Troublesome Nature of a Threshold Concept in Economics" (paper presented at the 10th Conference of the European Association for Research on Learning and Instruction [EARLI], Padova, Italy, August 26–30, 2003).

5. Jan H. F. Meyer, Ray Land, and Caroline Baillie, "Editors' Preface," in *Threshold Concepts and Transformational Learning*, ed. Jan H. F. Meyer, Ray Land, and Caroline Baillie, ix–xlii (Rotterdam, Netherlands: Sense Publishers, 2010).

6. Lori Townsend, Korey Brunetti, and Amy R. Hofer, "Threshold Concepts and Information Literacy," *portal: Libraries and the Academy* 11, no. 3 (July 2011): 853–69.

7. Association of College and Research Libraries, *Framework for Information Literacy for Higher Education*, 2.

8. Ibid., 10.

chapter 2

Scholarship as Conversation

"COMMUNITIES OF SCHOLARS, RESEARCHERS, OR PROFESSIONALS engage in sustained discourse with new insights and discoveries occurring over time as a result of varied perspectives and interpretations."[1] The phrase "scholarship as conversation" should be considered a metaphor for the give-and-take, point and counterpoint that are involved in a face-to-face, one-on-one conversation. In considering the metaphor, one can generalize from the in-person discussion at the water cooler to an online discussion that takes place across the world, synchronously or asynchronously, or that takes place more slowly as articles on a topic are published. Scholarship can and does emerge from private, face-to-face conversations, but those conversations are invisible to people who were not involved. Ideas from face-to-face conversations can have an impact on the development of new thinking. Their usefulness to research cannot be discounted. This utility is the most concrete aspect of a scholarly conversation.

The background work of scholarship involves many conversations. People get together and toss ideas around. They try new ideas by discussing them with friends and colleagues who are nearby. The researcher might reach out to others who have similar experience in the subject under study and exchange ideas by mail, through video chat, or at conferences. Scholars might form a working group to test ideas and have real-time conversations (or back-and-forth communication that is almost in real time) about what happened and why. Scholarship of this type takes place in what is called "the invisible college." It takes place among people who are working on a problem and is never recorded or released to the public. This limitation makes the conversation invisible to anyone who wasn't involved.

Using the metaphor "scholarship as conversation" beyond this point causes the metaphor to stretch the meaning of the word *conversation*. Published scholarship is

11

a pretty slow conversation. For example, an article is researched, written, submitted, vetted, and published. This process takes quite some time. Once an article is published, another scholar may use the information in it to research and publish a second article that might add to or refute all or part of the information in the first article. The first author may do more research based on the second author's work and publish a third article. Or a third author might take the work of the first two authors and create a third publication. Although this is a conversation of sorts, it is less flexible than a real conversation, and it takes much more time.

This slow conversation takes place on the pages of scholarly journals over a long period. The conversation does not take place in real time and does not provide the instant responses that are forthcoming in a face-to-face conversation. The time it takes to do research (gather information, conduct an experiment, assess the result, publish the findings, etc.) does not allow the conversation to happen in real time. The conversation develops slowly, giving researchers plenty of time to think about their response. In fact, the process takes so long that the first author might no longer be alive by the time the second author produces the second article. This means that continuing the conversation might not include the first author at all! This type of scholarly conversation may consist of a string of authors who were never able to respond to each other even though everyone was working and writing on the same topic.

If we look at the study of something through time, we can gather a history of research on the subject and see how the topic has developed. This effort amounts to gathering the complete transcript of the written conversation on the topic. To gather this conversation one could do a Google search on the topic and follow the links or find a blog or discussion board about the topic. One could gather parts of the conversation from journal articles, which often include a literature review. The literature review in a scholarly journal cites the most prominent references on the subject and provides the reader with a bibliographic history of scholarly research in the field. As new information becomes available, the literature reviews become longer or focus on one specific aspect of the topic. In any case, by looking at the references in any article, the reader can work backward in time to create a complete history of the written study of the topic. This activity amounts to the discovery of the published "conversation" that has taken place concerning the topic in question. This scholarly conversation has been recorded for others to use for their own education or to continue the research (add to the conversation) on the topic. One benefit of this published conversation is that the conversation is recoverable, unlike the "invisible college" conversation that disappears as it happens.

It is useful to be able to compile a history of the research on a particular topic—to gather the pieces of the written conversation that has already happened. Rather than having to reinvent and rediscover what other researchers have already found, a new researcher can see what progress has been made and start from where the last researcher left off, rather than starting from the beginning. The new researcher can also find out what work did or did not produce positive results. For example, a new researcher might be interested in studying the effect of turmeric on arthritis. By reviewing the literature, the researcher can determine whether someone else has already done some work on the connection between turmeric and arthritis, what that experiment was, and how it worked out. The new researcher can determine whether the previous researcher found a link or no link between turmeric and arthritis. If a link was found, the new researcher can try to replicate the original study, try a new angle on the old study, or decide to study something entirely different based on the outcome of the original research. Performing a literature review can also be useful in identifying areas of inquiry that have not yet been researched at all.

The study of the development of the scholarship about a topic will show the range and scope of the topic and how it has been approached. For example, using the topic of turmeric, a spice often used in Indian food, one finds many different uses for the spice. Turmeric has been used in cooking for ages, so information about such use is one facet of the research that is available. There are also many ideas about medical uses for turmeric. The medical literature about turmeric will be another facet of the research that is available. Turmeric used in art and ritual would also be facets of scholarship on the topic. The research and writing about each of these specific uses of turmeric are their own conversations. Adding together all the different conversations about turmeric gives the new researcher a sense of the scope of the conversation. Sometimes getting the big picture allows the researcher to make a connection or a mental leap to some new way of looking at the topic.

Conversations that take place in today's online environment differ in many ways from the conversations that took place before computers were available. Today the number and type of people who can be part of a conversation are not limited by geography. The physical location of individuals is no longer a barrier to conversation, as long as Internet access is available. There are news feeds, blogs, interest groups, clubs, and so on about almost any topic imaginable, so there are plenty of opportunities for individuals to be part of the conversation about almost any topic. This technology allows people who have something to add or who have questions about a topic to participate to an extent that was not available to them in the past. Economic restrictions are less of a barrier today as well. Researchers do not need to have inordinate amounts of money or equipment to gain access to the conversations taking place around the world. Although information is not free, the cost of participating in the conversation has become manageable for a large portion of the world's population, and the conversation itself can happen more quickly than in the past.

The scholarly world still has some specific ways of communicating information. The peer-reviewed journal is one example of a specific means of communicating ideas. This type of publication screens scholars and experts and eliminates those authors who do not have the credentials needed to contribute to a highly technical discussion. It allows only the privileged few who are experts in the field under consideration to speak on the subject. The experts on the topic speak to each other, because the articles in peer-re-viewed scholarly journals are most often geared toward other experts in the field. This type of publication doesn't usually appeal to outsiders, nor does it let outsiders become part of the conversation.

On the other hand, this type of conversation is useful to practitioners and special-ists in a field, because it allows them to make assumptions about what their colleagues already know. The conversation does not have to start at the very beginning but can pick up at a more advanced level and continue from that point. The very basic back-ground information does not need to be included in the conversation between schol-ars, and the older material concerning the topic can simply be referenced (rather than explained) because most scholars will already know this background material. This type of restricted conversation can help produce productive ideas more quickly.

In the Internet-based version of the academy, experts and scholars embrace many of the new opportunities for conversation as well. Experts can work together on ideas without the geographic and time constraints of the pre-computer world. Technology allows access to the discussion in various formats—blogs, newsfeeds, user groups, forums, and so on. People from different groups and backgrounds can be part of the process, even if they are not experts. People can share their ideas and questions more openly and quickly than in days past. Those outside the academy with an interest in the topic can be part of the conversation and can contribute their thoughts and ideas. This inclusion widens the scope of participation and improves the possibilities for new ideas and points of view.

As always, because almost anyone can become part of the new kind of scholarly conversation online, it is very important to think about both the information being conveyed and the person conveying the information. Not everyone who might weigh in on a topic online will be an expert. Some will have a better understanding of the topic than others. Some may have no understanding at all. Although the online conversation that is open to the public is richer and more diverse, it may require more evaluation by the participants. Evaluation of information is a vital part of both critical thinking and information literacy and is extremely important when scholarly credentials are not required for participation.

Internet-published scholarship must be carefully evaluated. As with those who com-ment on a subject on a blog or a forum, those who publish information on the open web may or may not have the expertise or training to provide accurate and reliable infor-mation. Publishers may or may not have established standards of quality for what they publish. The author and the publisher may be the same person. Online publishers may publish almost anything, written by almost anyone. This ability makes them part of the conversation, even if their contribution to the conversation is limited. It becomes the job of the information seeker to evaluate the information found on the open web, because the traditional means of filtering to eliminate unreliable information (editing or peer review, for example) are often not available on the Internet. The time needed to evaluate each piece of information and each person providing that information is a cost to consider.

A human trait that makes the scholarly conversation difficult is bias. What happens when you have a bias about a topic? If you feel strongly one way or the other about gun control or abortion, does the information you select about the topic reflect your opinions, rather than reflecting the facts? Does your interpretation of information about gun control or abortion depend on the opinions you already hold about the topic? Does what you write or say about that topic reflect that bias? Does the bias have an effect on the information you offer? Bias is a very human condition. It is difficult to dispense with one's own opinions altogether, and it is difficult to keep those opinions from coloring (consciously or unconsciously) the conversations we have. Information literacy should instruct students to be self-aware and to use self-awareness to counteract bias.

An interesting psychological phenomenon known as confirmation bias indicates that people who believe something tend to seek out information that supports that belief, rather than looking for information that refutes or contradicts that belief. We interpret information so that it will support our chosen point of view, even when that interpretation is not accurate. This tendency is something to be aware of when learning to be information literate. If confirmation bias is understood as a potential research hazard, students can make more effort to research the side of a conversation they do not support. Again, self-awareness is key.

Let's say a congressman is also a supporter of the right to bear arms. Would this congressman's bias be likely to influence his vote on gun control? Would he be more likely to spend time considering the information supplied by a pro–gun control lobbyist or an anti–gun control lobbyist? Would he be more likely to interpret data to fit his views? If he is typical, the congressman likely would seek out, select, and interpret information that supports what he already believes and would cast his vote based on his newly confirmed belief in the right to bear arms.

Confirmation bias looks for ideas and opinions that support information we already believe. Research that truly moves scholarship forward cannot be based on information that only supports or confirms what has gone before or that only supports the side of the question one agrees with. Scholarship must challenge what has gone before, and consider all points of view, in order to move forward. The tendency toward confirmation bias makes this a difficult task. This is why it is so important that outsiders be able to enter the conversation. All sides of a question need to be addressed with equal rigor in order to come to a logical conclusion. Information literacy instruction that includes self-checks and monitoring of thought processes can help to counteract confirmation bias.

Many medical doctors study cancer. Doctors are highly educated individuals who are experts and authorities on health and disease. Do the organizations they work for have an influence on their medical opinions? Consider the doctors who work for a nonprofit organization that studies cancer in the United States. The mission of the organization controls the research these doctors do. Then consider the doctors who work for a company that produces cigarettes. The mission of this company would not promote medical research that linked cigarettes with cancer. The research by doctors who work for the cigarette company will reflect the mission of the company. Although both organizations employ highly educated medical experts, the conclusions those experts come to in studies about lung cancer may be very different. The differences may be based on confirmation bias, or the source of a paycheck, or both.

In a sense it is here that input into the conversation from those outside the discipline in question may be most useful. Scholars inside a discipline have reached particular conclusions or beliefs based on much study and many years of work. They have time and effort invested in the ideas and opinions they support. This makes it hard to remain objective and to seek out and consider other ideas and conclusions. Those who are not specialists in a field may be less entrenched on one side of a question. They have less time and effort invested and may be able to consider many sides of a question more easily. This freedom to see multiple views in a scholarly conversation must be weighed against the outsider's relative lack of information and training in the subject area in question. Fortunately, in today's world of scholarship there is both room and opportunity for insiders and outsiders to address questions of interest.

NOTE

1. Association of College and Research Libraries, *Framework for Information Literacy for Higher Education* (Chicago: American Library Association, 2015), www.ala.org/acrl/standards/ilframework.

Informal Conversations

LEARNING OUTCOMES

- Students will be able to locate blogs on a specific topic.
- Students will learn how topics on a blog develop.
- Students will understand that a blog is a conversation, one way of having a sustained discourse among a group of people.

The instructor should select a number of controversial topics and allow students to select the topic that interests them the most. The instructor will provide students with two blogs for each topic, each blog offering a different point of view. Blogs should be active and have regular and frequent postings. Students should use each blog's archive to read postings from the past.

INSTRUCTIONS

Read the postings from two blogs concerning your chosen topic. Then answer the following questions:

What is the purpose for each blog?
- Blog 1
- Blog 2

Does the blog concern itself only with your chosen topic, or does it cover other subjects, too?
- Blog 1
- Blog 2

Who is the author of the blog, and what credentials does the blogger have?
- Blog 1
- Blog 2

Do the author's credentials convince you that the writer is an expert on the topic in question?
- Blog 1
- Blog 2

How many postings are there on your topic?
- Blog 1
- Blog 2

Are the ideas presented supported with evidence?
- Blog 1
- Blog 2

Does the blogger cite other writers or researchers?
- Blog 1
- Blog 2

Do people who comment on postings generally agree or disagree with the blogger?
- Blog 1
- Blog 2

Does either blog consider or mention the other's arguments concerning the topic?
- Blog 1
- Blog 2

Describe how the conversation on a blog might move scholarship about a topic forward.
- Blog 1
- Blog 2

Summarize what you have learned about blogs, bloggers, and the topic you selected.

Do you still have questions about your topic?

EXERCISE 2

Conversations between Experts

LEARNING OUTCOMES

- Students will learn how conversations about a topic of interest help develop ideas about that topic.
- Students will learn one means for having a slow conversation about a topic.
- Students will learn to consider how conversation moves knowledge forward.

The instructor should provide letters written between experts who carry on a conversation about a particular topic (for example, letters between Benjamin Franklin and John Adams or between Mark Twain and Ulysses Grant).

INSTRUCTIONS

Read the letters provided by your instructor and answer the following questions:

How long did it take to have this conversation?

What was the central topic?

Were new ideas discussed?

Were old ideas challenged?

Did the authors agree or disagree?

Did either author change the other's mind?

Did either author demonstrate any overt bias about the topic?

Did either author say anything you know to be untrue?

Was there an "aha" moment discussed by either author? (Did either author suddenly understand the topic or the other person's point of view?)

Could the conversation have had an impact on the later work of the people involved?

How did the social history of the time during which the authors were writing affect the discussion?

What was going on in the world at that time?

Identifying Most Important or Most Cited Information

LEARNING OUTCOMES

- Students will be able to summarize information presented in a current article.
- Students will be able to locate and examine the bibliography of an article.
- Students will be able to describe how a chain of research is created over time.
- Students will be able to identify the most important information about a topic.

The instructor should guide the class through this exercise. The instructor should select a current topic that has been the subject of ongoing research—a medical breakthrough, global warming, obesity, and the like. The instructor should provide the students with a copy of a current research paper (or a link to an article). To save time, the instructor might assign the first article to be read before presenting this exercise. The instructor should also provide copies of or links to the other articles in the exercise. This exercise works well in a computer classroom where students can all look at the same screens.

INSTRUCTIONS

Read the supplied article noting any conclusions reached. Then answer the following questions:

What topic is the author reporting on?

Does the author include a section in the article describing the research done previously on the same topic?

Does the author include a bibliography?

What conclusion does the author come to?

Does the author answer the research question?

Examine the bibliography for the article.

How many citations does the bibliography contain?

What is the date of the oldest publication cited in the bibliography?

What is the date of the newest publication cited in the bibliography?

Find the most current article or book or report listed in the bibliography of the first article by looking at the dates of publication. Skim the second article.

Is the topic of the second article exactly the same as the first?

If not, how are the two articles different?

Does the author of the second article include a literature review?

Does the author answer the research question?

How many items are listed in the second bibliography?

What is the date of the oldest publication cited in the bibliography?

What is the date of the newest publication cited in the bibliography?

Look at the bibliographies for both articles.

How many of the citations are the same in both bibliographies?

Select the most current article or book or report from the bibliography of the second article by looking at the dates of publication. Skim the third article.

Is the topic of the third article exactly the same as the topic of the second article?

If not, how are the two articles different?

Does the author of the third article include a literature review?

Does the author answer the question posed in the article?

How many items are listed in the third bibliography?

What is the date of the oldest publication cited in the bibliography?

What is the date of the newest publication cited in the bibliography?

Examine the bibliographies for the second and third articles.

How many of the citations are the same?

Are there any articles that appear in the bibliographies of all three articles?

What conclusions can you draw about the importance of the articles that keep appearing in research on this topic?

Can you follow changes in the thinking about the topic over time, based on the focus of the three articles you looked at?

How far back in time could you follow this topic? How?

EXERCISE 4

Bias

LEARNING OUTCOMES

- Students will be able to define bias.
- Students will be able to detect bias.
- Students will be able to link sources of information with possible bias.

Students may complete this exercise individually or in pairs. The instructor may supply additional pairs of websites that offer opposing points of view on a topic. The instructor should provide the definition of *bias:*

1. A particular tendency, trend, inclination, feeling, or opinion, especially one that is preconceived or unreasoned: illegal bias against older job applicants; the magazine's bias toward art rather than photography; our strong bias in favor of the idea.
2. Unreasonably hostile feelings or opinions about a social group; prejudice: accusations of racial bias. (www.dictionary.reference.com)

INSTRUCTIONS

Go to the following websites and read the mission statement for both organizations.

- www.nrlc.org
- www.plannedparenthood.org

What is the stated purpose of each organization?

Now look at the information given about the topic of abortion at each website and answer the following questions:

- www.nrlc.org/education/
- www.plannedparenthood.org/learn/abortion

How much information about abortion does the NRLC provide?

How much information about Planned Parenthood does the NRLC convey?

How much information about abortion does Planned Parenthood provide?

How much information about the NRLC does Planned Parenthood provide?

What conclusions can be drawn from the amount and type of information each organization provides about abortion?

How does the purpose of each organization affect the information it provides at its website?

EXERCISE 5

Evaluation of Sources

It doesn't matter whether the search for information is for personal reasons or is work related. When using the Internet to identify information that addresses a problem, concern, or question, all information must be evaluated.

LEARNING OUTCOMES

- Students will be able to evaluate information found on the Internet.
- Students will be able to determine the value of the information based on their evaluation.

The instructor should have students evaluate two websites on the same topic. Students will answer all the questions for both websites and then compare the two websites to select the "best" website (i.e., the one that provides the best answers to the questions posed).

INSTRUCTIONS

Examine each website and answer the following questions for each site:

Who is the author of the information?

What expertise does the author have?

Is the author's expertise relevant to the topic of discussion? (Is the author talking about her field of expertise?)

What organization is sponsoring the provision of the information (e.g., website, blog, forum, journal, etc.)?

What is the website's domain (e.g., .com, .org, .edu, etc.)?

Is the information accurate?

How do you know?

Is the information up to date?

How do you know?

Can you tell where the information came from? (What sources were used to gather the information for the website?)

Is there a bibliography?

Is the information biased or misleading in any way?

Is the information presented as fact or opinion?

Has the website been updated recently?

Comparing your answers for both websites, which of the two websites would be most valuable in providing an answer to a research question?

Why?

SAMPLE PAIRS OF WEBSITES

Websites about Martin Luther King Jr.

- www.martinlutherking.org
- The Martin Luther King, Jr. Research and Education Institute: https://kinginstitute.stanford.edu

Websites about cloning

- Clonaid: www.clonaid.com
- Human Cloning Foundation: www.humancloning.org

Websites about UFOs

- FBI Records: The Vault—UFO: https://vault.fbi.gov/UFO
- UFO Evidence: www.ufoevidence.org

Websites about President Barack Obama

- The White House—President Barack Obama: www.whitehouse.gov/administration/president-Obama
- Organizing for Action: www.barackobama.com

EXERCISE 6

Comparing Information

Students should consider the ideas of more than one person about a topic. To gain an understanding of a topic, they must learn enough about it to know what the "middle of the road" is and what ideas might be out on the fringes.

LEARNING OUTCOMES

- Students will learn to gather information to gain a general sense of the range of belief on a topic.
- Students will evaluate information offered by different authors on a topic.
- Students will select the "best" information by comparing evaluations.

The instructor should provide links to three speeches given by three different politicians on a controversial topic—gun control or taxes, for example. One politician should be from the right, one from the left, and one centrist.

INSTRUCTIONS

Read the speeches and answer the following questions:

Is this author for or against the topic (gun control, federal taxes, etc.)?
- Author 1
- Author 2
- Author 3

What are the author's main arguments?
- Author 1
- Author 2
- Author 3

Does the author provide any facts? If so, where do those facts come from?
- Author 1
- Author 2
- Author 3

Does the author take an all-or-nothing stand on the issue?
- Author 1
- Author 2
- Author 3

Is the difference between the authors' stands on the issue wide or narrow?

Is a middle-of-the-road position possible?

Is one author's argument more compelling than the others' arguments? If so, why?

Evaluating Different Types of Information Sources

LEARNING OUTCOMES

- Students will learn about different information sources.
- Students will learn how information sources differ from one another.
- Students will learn to select the sources that fulfill the information need.

The instructor should provide several articles about a topic: one article from a newspaper, one from a magazine, and one from a scholarly journal.

INSTRUCTIONS

Fill out the following worksheet to compare the information from each source.

	Newspaper	Magazine	Journal
Author			
Author's Credentials			
Publisher Purpose for Information Source			
Date of Article			
Article Length			
Facts			
Opinions			
Data/Statistics			
Conclusions			

Bibliography			
Other Sources Cited			

To identify the most accurate and reliable source, answer the following questions:

Which source gave the most information?

Did all sources supply the same facts?

Did all sources supply the same number of facts?

Did all sources come to the same conclusions?

Were all authors experts on the topic?

Did the authors cite the sources of their information?

Did the articles include a bibliography?

What is the purpose for each type of information source (newspaper, magazine, journal)?

Which source would provide the best information for scholarly work?

Which source would provide the best information for a current events report?

Sources That Disagree

What should students do when sources disagree?

LEARNING OUTCOMES

- Students will learn how to evaluate sources.
- Students will learn to consider differences and disagreements in scholarship.
- Students will learn to apply evaluative criteria to arguments to determine the validity of each side.

The instructor should provide articles that discuss the same topic but come to different conclusions (e.g., an NRA publication and a gun control publication; proponents and opponents of the Affordable Care Act; a Republican and a Democrat, etc.).

INSTRUCTIONS

Read two articles from opposing sources and answer the following questions:

Who are the authors and what are their credentials?

What is each publication and what is its mission?

What is the argument?

How do the two sides differ?

Are the facts they present different?

Do both sides consider the same factors?

Do both sides show where their information came from?

Is the question legitimately open to interpretation?

EXERCISE 9

Confirmation Bias

LEARNING OUTCOMES

- Students will learn that there are at least two sides to any argument.
- Students will learn that studying one side of an argument will result in learning only about that side of the argument.
- Students will learn that researching all sides of a controversial topic will inform their arguments.

The instructor should have students form two teams. Using a debate question supplied by the instructor, one half of the class should take the "pro" side and one half of the class should address the "con" side of the argument.

INSTRUCTIONS

Gather information about the question. Create a bibliography of sources you find. Answer the following questions and discuss the results:

How much information did you find that supported your side of the argument?

How much information did you find that supported the other side of the argument?

Did you use any of the information that did not support your side of the argument?

Would you be able to win the debate using the information you gathered?

To refute the other side of an argument, you have to know what that side is and what information that side of the argument is based on. If you ignore the information that doesn't agree with what you think or expect, you will find only the information that confirms what you think or expect.

Confronting Confirmation Bias

LEARNING OUTCOMES

- Students will learn how confirmation bias colors research results.
- Students will learn about their own confirmation bias.

The instructor should allow students to select their own topics for this exercise.

INSTRUCTIONS

Select a controversial issue and state which side of the controversy you agree with and why. Find at least three articles that support the other side of the argument and answer the following questions:

What reasons do the authors give for taking this side in the argument?

Did you learn anything new about the topic?

Did the authors offer any ideas you had not heard before?

Did you learn anything about the people who support the other side of the argument?

Did you change your mind or soften your personal position as a result of reading the three articles?

Did you discover any holes in your own side of the argument?

Did you discover that any of the ideas on either side of the argument need more investigation?

Did you discover any confirmation bias in yourself?

Changing Course

LEARNING OUTCOMES

- Students will learn that new discoveries and new views can change the conversation.
- Students will learn that what we thought we knew can change in a scholarly conversation.
- Students will investigate the history of sugar in the diet.

The instructor should provide copies of the following article: Gary Taubes, "Is Sugar Toxic?" *New York Times Magazine*, April 13, 2011, www.nytimes.com/2011/04/17/magazine/mag-17Sugar-t.html?_r=0.

INSTRUCTIONS

Using Taubes's article concerning sugar, and any other relevant information you need, answer the following questions:

Does Gary Taubes have a degree in any discipline related to the topic?

Does Gary Taubes propose a hypothesis about sugar in the human diet?

Does Taubes review the literature about the topic?

Does Taubes make legitimate claims about the research studies he references?

Does Taubes use the existing research to support his hypothesis?

Does Taubes provide new information?

Does the new information change how researchers might look at the topic in the future?

chapter 3

Research as Inquiry

"**R**ESEARCH IS ITERATIVE AND DEPENDS UPON ASKING INCREASINGLY complex or new questions whose answers in turn develop additional questions or lines of inquiry in any field."[1] Lane Wilkinson, reference and instruction librarian at the University of Tennessee at Chattanooga and contributor to the *Sense and Reference* blog, makes the distinction between *search* and *research*: "When you know the answer, or know that an answer exists, you search. When you don't know the answer, or aren't even sure about the question, you research."[2] Some Internet tools are very good at searching. Google, for example, is a very good place to look when searching for information that is known: Who is the president of France? What is the population of Montana? How do I grow heirloom tomatoes? All these questions can be answered easily by using a search engine. Students (and many, many others) frequently start and finish their search with Google. In many cases, this tool is all that is necessary. However, when doing research, Google is not enough.

Wilkinson goes on to say, "There's a big difference between where you start your research and where you end it. . . . Novice researchers tend to start in Google and stay in Google."[3] Failing to go beyond Google is a problem when thinking about research—about questions that may not have answers. Novices do not necessarily search for tools beyond Google, even when they are trying to find information that might help answer a complex question. In order to grasp the concept of research as inquiry, students must understand that any one tool—Google or any other search engine—is not enough by itself. It might be a starting point, but in order to move toward answering new questions, more is needed.

FROM SEARCH TO RESEARCH

Research involves asking new questions and seeking answers by combining and recombining facts and information pulled from a variety of sources. Research requires thought, reflection, inspiration, uncertainty, and tenacity. It involves the understanding that everything is *not* known and that new knowledge can be created by asking new questions and seeking answers to those questions. Research also involves the understanding that inquiry can be useful and productive even if definitive answers to the research question are not found.

Students should be encouraged to ask questions. They should come to understand that research is often based on asking new questions about research that has already been done. Very few topics are closed to further investigation. The first person to investigate a topic or idea does not usually start at zero. There is always something already known about the topic that causes the person to wonder or speculate about the topic or about something related, either directly or by metaphor.

The person who first thought about the idea of sound waves, for example, may have based those thoughts on what was known about waves in water. The first person to wonder what causes waves in water may have based that question on water in a still pond. The first person to wonder about how water gets into a pond may have based that question on information about melting glaciers. The point is that from existing information, new questions can emerge. By attempting to answer those questions, people create new information. New information builds on existing information. Sometimes ideas are directly linked and progress logically from step 1 to step 2. Other ideas involve a kind of mental leap to get from the established knowledge to the new knowledge. In either case, the process starts with something known and moves toward something unknown.

Much of students' school time is spent memorizing or understanding known information. In fact, students often begin to think that everything is already known and that their job is simply to learn it. They get so busy memorizing that they often stop asking questions. They memorize rather than understand. They recite rather than explain. The incessant *why* questions of the toddler disappear over time. Teachers are often rushed for time to cover their subject matter. There is often not enough time to fully consider all the questions that students might have. The ability to question the authority of a fact or a history is trained out of students as they progress through the school system until they feel they cannot ask any question, even if they know how. Then when they get to college or enter the workforce, they are expected to know how to ask and answer questions, even though many of them are long out of practice. This expectation often surprises students because their school experiences may well have trained them not to ask questions or question information. One job of information literacy is to help students relearn the art of asking questions. Our success or failure in this endeavor has long-term implications in the larger world.

In helping create lifelong learners and critical thinkers, the educational setting should be the place where students gain experience in forming and asking questions. They should understand that not every question has a known answer. They should learn that not every question has a right or a wrong answer. They should learn that challenging existing information is a way of asking a new question. They should learn that known information can be revisited when new knowledge comes to light. They should learn that new ideas can be applied to known information to create new knowledge. They should learn that they might be the person who eventually answers the question that has no answer today.

FROM TOPIC TO RESEARCH QUESTION

For students, inquiry often begins when they are given a general topic and are asked to design an inquiry relating to that topic. Many students have no idea how to get from the general topic to a specific question about that topic. They often do not understand that a general topic is too large to investigate in any reasonable time frame. They have little or no experience in narrowing their scope from a general topic to a research question. One part of the problem is that students who are novice researchers often do not know much about the topic they have been assigned. Another part of the problem is that students have not been guided through the process of creating a research question, nor have they practiced doing so. They are not knowledgeable about how to connect research methods to a research question, nor are they knowledgeable enough to know what questions have already been asked and what questions might be new. Finally, most students feel that if they pose a research question and fail to answer it, they have failed. They would much rather confirm the question they pose than answer it negatively or not at all. Students therefore often pose research questions whose answers they already know (or think they already know).

Students are often given some choice when instructors assign a paper or project. This option allows students to select a question of interest to them. This personal interest sustains them through the research and writing process. However, it also proves problematic for many students because it doesn't offer enough guidance about how to get from the general assignment to a specific question or proposition that the student can research. The information literacy instructor should create the opportunity to practice getting from a topic to a research question.

If the assignment is to write a paper on a topic of personal interest that relates to American history from 1620 to 1776, a student might have difficulty coming up with a topic. In addition, a topic that applies to the time period may still be too big to cover in the context of a term paper, a presentation, an essay, or whatever the assignment parameters might be. For example, a student decides the topic of interest to her is life in the Plymouth Colony. This is a good starting point, but a ten-page paper about life in the Plymouth Colony would be very general and not very interesting because the topic is too vast. The topic does not ask a question, nor does it seek out new knowledge. Providing students with opportunities to practice narrowing a topic will improve their overall success with a research project.

Students find it very difficult to narrow a topic to a concept or time frame appropriate to the scope of their assignment. If they do manage to narrow their topic, it is even harder for them to restate that narrower topic as a research question. It is in this process that information literacy instruction can be helpful. By guiding students through the process and giving them examples of how they might narrow a topic, instructors can help students understand the process of matching a topic to the scope of an assignment. Then as students receive guidance and feedback while creating questions based on their narrowed topics, the job becomes more familiar and more manageable for them.

It is often useful to start a lesson with an example that is already familiar to students. A second example can then be introduced with an explanation of how it is like the first example. This process creates a mental link between the two examples. When the student thinks about the first example, the second example will come to mind. This process of linking can be applied with any number of relevant examples. Each repetition of the linking process makes the concept clearer. Once the concept is understood, it is then much easier to apply it to a new situation. Supplying increasingly varied examples (starting with the most similar and working toward the most disparate) will improve the ability of the student to think outside the box when making connections between the known and the unknown. Having students learn by analogy helps them retain what they have learned and makes it easier for them to retrieve the information when it is needed.

Students often approach research without much thought or planning. Thinking about a topic, writing down ideas, and organizing the ideas is a good mental exercise that can result in a representation of what one knows and, by default, what one doesn't know about a topic. Students should be encouraged to plot their ideas on paper or on the computer. By jotting down ideas, students can help themselves divide large topics into smaller ones. They can make connections between topics that might not have been obvious when simply thinking about those topics. Students can see some ideas develop as they rearrange the pieces they have written down. Brainstorming is a very productive way of producing ideas. Writing down those ideas in some fashion helps make them visible rather than virtual. They can be moved and rearranged into clusters or compared and contrasted. Whether using an outline or a concept map, on paper or electronically, students will find that this practice is a good way to organize ideas for consideration.

NOTES

1. Association of College and Research Libraries, *Framework for Information Literacy for Higher Education* (Chicago: American Library Association, 2015).

2. Lane Wilkinson, "Is Research Inquiry?" *Sense and Reference: A Philosophical Library Blog,* July 15, 2014, https://senseandreference.wordpress.com/2014/07/15/is-research -inquiry.

3. Wilkinson, "Is Research Inquiry?"

EXERCISE 12

Buying a Cell Phone: Narrowing the Options

By the time they get to college, most students have purchased a cell phone. There are thousands of different kinds of phones. If students simply walk into a store and purchase a phone, they will have accomplished their task, but they may not get the phone they really need or want. By asking a series of questions before buying a phone, students can narrow their options to the point at which they can make an informed decision.

LEARNING OUTCOMES

- Students will learn how to ask questions about a topic.
- Students will learn how to narrow their topic based on the answers to the questions.

The instructor may choose any complex process that can be simplified by narrowing choices—planning a European vacation, choosing a college, buying a car, and the like.

INSTRUCTIONS

Imagine you want to buy a cell phone. To make an informed decision, begin by answering the following questions:

What do you need the phone for? List all the things you want to do with your phone.
- Voice
- Internet
- Pictures
- GPS
- Music
- Special apps
- Other

If you need all these features in a phone, then you can ignore any models that don't have these features. This narrows your choices.

How often will you be using your phone?
- 24/7?
- Any time you are not sleeping?
- Only during your free time?

If you will be using your phone every waking hour of the day, you will want to get the phone with the longest lasting battery or the quickest recharge time, or both. You will want a phone that you can charge from a wall outlet or from a car or other charger. Any phone that does not have the battery life or the charging options needed can be eliminated. This narrows your choices.

What devices will your phone replace?
- Camera
- Desktop computer
- Calculator
- iPod
- Other

If you will be using the phone exclusively for all of the above (that is, you will not use computers, tablets, or other devices to do some of your work), you will want a phone that has a good reliability rating, a long-lasting battery, a quick-charge capability, and a size that will allow you to do all your work. You can eliminate all phones that do not have a large display, for example. This narrows your choices.

Are you likely to use the phone hard or gently?

If you are the kind of person who tends to stick your phone in the top of your boot and then go wading, or the kind of person who tries to carry everything at once and consequently drops things regularly, you will want to consider only those phones that are rugged or encased in a strong cover. You can eliminate all phones that are delicate or phones that need to be used ever so carefully. This narrows your choices.

Do you (or does your family) have a calling plan?

Does that plan limit you in the phones you can use?

If so, you don't need to look at any others. This narrows your choices.

How good a camera do you need?
- Will you be taking pictures that need to be publishable?
- Is the picture quality vital to your work?

You will only need to look at phones with suitable camera capability. This narrows your choices.

What price range are you considering?

If your budget allows you to spend only $100 for a phone, you won't need to consider anything that costs more than $100. This narrows your choices.

When you have answered all the questions you can think of about the phone you want, write a short paragraph that summarizes what you will be looking for. (For example, I want a phone on which I can call, text, access the Internet, take pictures, play music, and navigate. I need a rugged phone, and I will probably want screen replacement or repair insurance. I want a phone that will be supported by my family calling plan. I want a phone with an excellent camera. I have a budget of $500.)

Once you have collected all this information, you are ready to start looking for a specific phone. From the millions of phones available, you can limit your search by asking a few questions. If you ask those questions before you start looking at phones, you can focus your search considerably and spend your time looking only at phones that meet your criteria. Many times we go through this process without thinking about it. When it comes to research, using this process will have the same time-saving result.

Narrowing a Topic

LEARNING OUTCOMES

- Students will learn to ask questions about a topic to identify subdivisions of that topic.
- Students will learn to seek background information on a topic to identify subdivisions of that topic.
- Students will learn how to formulate a research question from a narrowed topic.

The instructor may want to lead students through this exercise using a preselected topic. The exercise can be broken into several sessions if necessary.

INSTRUCTIONS: PART 1

Imagine you want to do research about life in the Plymouth Colony. Begin by answering the following questions:

What dates do you want to consider? Only 1620? Do you want to investigate a range of dates? Do you want to compare life in the colony at one date with life in the colony at another date?

Whose life do you want to consider (e.g., only men, only women, everyone)?

Do you want to consider the interactions between groups (e.g., men and women, Native Americans and colonists, parents and children)?

How do you define *life*? There is a lot to living every day. Do you want to know about how houses were built? Do you want to know about what food was available? Do you want to know what political system was used? Do you want to know how clothing was made?

How long is your paper supposed to be (e.g., ten pages, two pages)?

What kinds of sources are you required to use (e.g., primary or secondary, scholarly)? Is there any type of source you may not use?

INSTRUCTIONS: PART 2

Encyclopedias give information about subjects or topics. They divide the large subject into smaller subtopics to explain relevant ideas associated with the big topic. When looking for ideas about how to outline or map a topic, it's often useful to go to an encyclopedia article and see how the article is subdivided. What subtopics are covered in the article? *Wikipedia* (https://en.wikipedia.org/wiki/Plymouth_Colony) breaks up the article about the Plymouth Colony like this:

1 History
    1.1 Origins
    1.2 *Mayflower* voyage
    1.3 Prior exploration and settlements
    1.4 Landings at Provincetown and Plymouth
    1.5 First winter
    1.6 "First Thanksgiving"
    1.7 Early relations with the Native Americans
    1.8 Growth of Plymouth
    1.9 Military history
        1.9.1 Myles Standish
        1.9.2 Pequot War
        1.9.3 King Philip's War
    1.10 Final years

2 Life
    2.1 Religion
    2.2 Marriage and family life
    2.3 Childhood, adolescence, and education

3 Government and laws
    3.1 Organization
    3.2 Laws
    3.3 Official Seal

4 Geography
    4.1 Boundaries
    4.2 Counties and towns

5 Demographics
    5.1 English
    5.2 Native Americans
    5.3 Black slaves

6 Economy

7 Legacy
    7.1 Art, literature, and film
    7.2 Thanksgiving
    7.3 Plymouth Rock
    7.4 Political legacy
    7.5 The Mayflower Society

8 See also
    8.1 Locations related to Plymouth Colony
    8.2 Monuments and other commemorations

9 Notes

10 References

11 External links

Use a *general encyclopedia* to look up your general topic. Examine the article about your topic. List the headings and subheadings in the article. Identify subheadings that are of interest to you. Check the end of the article for any citations to other books, articles, and the like about your area of interest. Ask yourself questions about what might be missing or incomplete. Are there other aspects of your topic that don't seem to be covered in the encyclopedia article? Are there links between items on the outline that bear further investigation?

Advanced students might want to look at an article on the same topic in a *subject-specific encyclopedia*. An encyclopedia of the history of colonial America, for example, would have more in-depth information about the Plymouth Colony. Again, locate the article and identify and mark subheadings that are of interest. Check the end of the article for further reading suggestions.

INSTRUCTIONS: PART 3
After thinking about and deciding what you are interested in writing about your topic, try putting a research question into words. Select two topics or subtopics and write a possible research question that links the two ideas. For example, if you are interested in colonial clothing, you might take the headings "colonial dress" and "women" to pose the question, "How did women in the Plymouth Colony make clothing during the first ten years?" If your interest is in the politics of the colony, you might take the headings "government and laws" and "voting" and pose a question such as, "How did decision making change in Plymouth Colony between 1620 and 1640?" If you are interested in the interactions between colonists and the Native Americans they met, you might link the headings "Native Americans" and "economy" and ask, "What role did Native Americans play in the successful establishment of the Plymouth Colony?" Notice that these questions cannot be answered yes or no.

Write two possible research questions concerning your topic.

EXERCISE 14

Creating a Concept Map

LEARNING OUTCOMES

- Students will learn how to create a concept map.
- Students will learn how to identify subtopics and topic-related ideas.
- Students will learn how to think about different facets of a topic and how parts might fit together into an interesting line of inquiry.

The instructor may wish to do a sample concept map with the entire class before having students try one on their own.

INSTRUCTIONS

In the middle of a large piece of paper, or using online concept mapping software (bubblus.com), write your general topic (see figure 3.1).

Around the central topic, write down as many subtopics as you can think of. You can add more as you go. This is brainstorming—there are no correct answers.

In circles around the subtopics, write down sub-subtopics.

Think about how subtopics and sub-subtopics might interconnect with each other. Draw lines between subtopics and sub-subtopics that seem related or about which you have questions and want to know more. (For example, you might connect *women* and *politics* and raise some questions at the intersection of the two topics.) Think of questions you might have about those connections. Put connected ideas or topics together in questions. Write two questions about connected ideas.

Figure 3.1
Concept Map

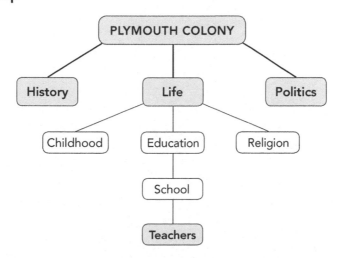

Do you already know the answers to your questions?

If yes, write the answer to one of your questions and ask another question based on that answer. For example, say your question was "What political offices were held by women at Plymouth Colony?" and you know that the answer is "Women were not allowed to hold political office at Plymouth Colony." You might then ask, "Since women were not allowed to hold political office at Plymouth Colony, how did they engage in the political processes that helped run the colony?"

Are there connections between questions that you might want to consider?

Formulate a question that sums up what you want to know about your subtopic or connected subtopics. (You may want to draw a second concept map with a subtopic at the center and repeat the process.)

EXERCISE 15

Creating an Outline

Some people would rather outline their ideas. The goals of an outline are similar to those of the concept map—to identify themes, ideas, and subtopics and to think about questions that might link those known ideas in new and interesting ways. To get an idea about what an outline looks like and how it can be used like a concept map, look at an encyclopedia or a writing handbook example of how to construct an outline. The following sources may be helpful:

> "Making an Outline," *Writing through Art* (May 2, 2012), www.youtube.com/watch?v=fCujEU6xZS0.
>
> "How to Write an Outline," *WikiHow to Do Anything,* www.wikihow.com/Write-an-Outline.

LEARNING OUTCOMES

- Students will learn how to create an outline.
- Students will learn about resources that can help them create an outline.
- Students will learn how to break a large topic into smaller subcategories.
- Students will learn how to formulate questions based on specific areas of interest about a general topic.

The instructor should lead the whole class through the first part of the exercise.

INSTRUCTIONS: PART 1

As a class, use *Wikipedia* or another encyclopedia to find an article on a topic of the instructor's choice. Examine the article to see how it is constructed. Identify the parts of the article and then write the parts on a flip chart or chalkboard. Note the structure of the article.

What subheadings are used?

How are those subheading topics written?

Are they broken down into sub-subtopics?

INSTRUCTIONS: PART 2

Work in small groups or individually. Following the structure of the outline created in the first part of the exercise, create an outline for your new topic, including the subtopics you can think of. Under each of the subtopics you have identified, list smaller subdivisions that could be discussed in each of the subtopics.

From your outline, select one or two subtopics you are interested in. Write a question that asks what you want to know about the subtopic. You may ask questions that combine aspects of more than one subtopic.

Look at the list of references at the end of the *Wikipedia* or other encyclopedia article.

Are there any references that might help you find more information on your question?

Where else might you look for information that will address your research question?

EXERCISE 16

Primary Sources

In an academic setting, many research tools often are available. Some tools are online, whereas others are available in paper format. Some tools deal with primary sources, and others deal with secondary sources. Some resources are general, and others are very specific. Students should be encouraged to explore a variety of information sources and discover the purpose for each. Knowing the scope and purpose for each type of source will help determine where the students look for information.

LEARNING OUTCOMES

- Students will learn what a primary source is.
- Students will learn where to look for primary source information.
- Students will learn some of the limitations and benefits of using primary sources.

The instructor will provide copies of primary sources, such as diaries, documents, transcripts of congressional hearings, and the like.

INSTRUCTIONS: PART 1

Working as a class, brainstorm answers for the following questions and write the answers on a flip chart or chalkboard.

What is a primary source?

Name some primary sources.

Where are primary sources found?

How would you search for a primary source in your library catalog?

What are the benefits of using a primary source?

What are some possible drawbacks of using primary sources?

INSTRUCTIONS: PART 2

Examine the contents of the primary source document provided by your instructor and answer the following questions:

Who wrote the document? (Name all known authors.)

What topic did the author or authors write about?

Where did the author or authors get the information?

Is there information in the document that you know to be true or false?

Is the document meant to be opinion or fact?

What does the document tell you about the person who wrote it?

What does the document tell you about the time during which the author lived?

Is there any particular motivation or bias evident in the document's contents?

INSTRUCTIONS: PART 3

Using the Internet or other search tools, answer the following questions:

Where can the original document be found?

Can one look at the original document?

What could you learn from the original document that you can't learn from a digitized or printed copy?

EXERCISE 17

Identifying Research Methods and Information Needs

LEARNING OUTCOMES

- Students will learn to consider what kind of resource might contain needed information.
- Students will learn to consider the scope of the research needed in conjunction with the types of information sources considered.

The instructor can assist with suggested types of information sources.

INSTRUCTIONS

For each of the following types of assignments, indicate what sources of information you would need and where you would find those sources. For example, if your assignment is to write an article for the school newspaper about the football game next Saturday, what information sources would you need and where are those sources located?

For a general term paper
- Information sources
- Location of sources

For a PhD dissertation
- Information sources
- Location of sources

For a report to a committee
- Information sources
- Location of sources

For a field report
- Information sources
- Location of sources

For a reflective journal entry
- Information sources
- Location of sources

For an oral history
- Information sources
- Location of sources

For a brochure for an organization
- Information sources
- Location of sources

EXERCISE 18

Who Would Know?

LEARNING OUTCOMES

- Students will learn to brainstorm about possible sources of information based on the question.
- Students will learn to look for possible sources of information based on the question.

The instructor could select questions either generally relevant to the students or specific to their geographic location or their major.

INSTRUCTIONS

List possible sources of answers for the following information needs:

> *Example:*
> *Information need:* Rules for obtaining a driver's license in Rhode Island
> *Sources of information:* Rhode Island Division of Motor Vehicles, Rhode Island statutes, American Automobile Association (AAA), driving school

Information need: Transportation from JFK Airport in New York City to Wall Street
Sources of information:

Information need: How to buy a cell phone app
Sources of information:

Information need: Causes of the U.S. Civil War
Sources of information:

Information need: Medical treatment for rheumatoid arthritis
Sources of information:

Information need: Effectiveness of standardized testing in schools in the United States
Sources of information:

Information need: Pros and cons of gun control
Sources of information:

EXERCISE 19

Creating a Research Question Is Research!

LEARNING OUTCOMES

- Students will learn that the first attempt to find information may not supply the information needed.
- Students will learn to combine and refine search terms.
- Students will learn that different resources may provide different answers to research questions.
- Students will learn that creating a research question is part of the research process.

This exercise can be done as a class, in small groups, or individually.

INSTRUCTIONS

First attempts to find information don't always pay off. Different disciplines can use the same word to mean different things. Use the Internet to search for information on the term "depression."

How many results did you get?

How many of these results could you reasonably look at?

How many of the sources listed on the first page of results are about mental depression?

Return to your search screen and search for "depression and economics."

How many results did you get?

How many of these could you reasonably look at?

Looking at the first page of results, is there any overlap with the first search?

If not, why not?

Return to your search screen and search for "depression and geology."

How many results did you get?

How many of these could you reasonably look at?

Do any of the sources on the first page from this search overlap with results of the previous two searches?

Return to your search screen and search for "depression and geology and United States."

How many results did you get?

How many of these could you reasonably look at?

How could you narrow your search more?

Return to your search screen and search for "depression and geology and sinkhole."

How many results did you get?

Did you find any articles that were about sinkholes outside the United States?

Return to your search screen and repeat your search using "depression and geology and sinkhole and Florida."

How many results did you get?

Now imagine that you have to write a research paper on this topic. Think about what you might want to know about sinkholes. Think about what you might want to know about sinkholes in Florida. Write a research question based on the geologic depression searching you have just done.

What is accomplished when you use additional terms to specify the information you are looking for?

What happens if you don't use additional terms to specify the information you are looking for?

How does it help to specify the discipline-specific use of the word you are searching?

EXERCISE 20

Asking Questions

LEARNING OUTCOMES

- Students will learn that one question leads to another.
- Students will learn to persist in asking questions.

The instructor should provide a list of questions about topics of interest. This exercise can be done as a class, in small groups, or individually.

INSTRUCTIONS

Use library resources, online resources, or both to answer the questions provided by your instructor. Use the following examples as a guide for the process.

Example: What is global warming?

Find a definition for the term. What source did you use?

Using the definition found, create a question about global warming.

Example: What causes global warming?

Find a list of possible causes of global warming. What source did you use?

Using one of the causes on the list, create a question about a cause of global warming.

Example: How does increased CO_2 contribute to global warming?

Find an article that answers the question.

From the article about how CO_2 contributes to global warming, create another question.

Example: How would planting more trees help control CO_2 levels?

Continue this process until you come up with a question that cannot be answered.

EXERCISE 21

Analogies

LEARNING OUTCOMES

- Students will learn to think broadly about how one thing might relate to or have similarities with something else.
- Students will learn to ask questions about what makes ideas similar or different.

This exercise can be done as a class, in small groups, or individually.

INSTRUCTIONS

Pairs of words in analogies have a relationship to each other. If you identify the relationship between the first pair of words, you can complete the second pair of words by applying the same relationship. For example, in the analogy "north is to south as east is to _____," the first pair of words are opposites. The opposite of "east" is the word that would fit the analogy. Complete the following analogous pairs:

Scissors is to cut as crayon is to _____.   Man is to woman as boy is to _____.

Road is to car as track is to _____.   Mountain is to high as valley is to _____.

Mother is to child as chicken is to _____.   Dove is to peace as hawk is to _____.

Verse is to song as chapter is to _____.

For the following pairs, list everything you can think of that makes them similar:

Example: Cat and dog
    Both are living; both are mammals; both are house pets; both are four-legged; both can be hunters; both have whiskers; both have footpads; both come in a large number of shapes, sizes, and colors; both are related to wild animals; both have canine teeth; and so on.

The United States and Vietnam   Physics and anthropology

Wool and cotton   Business and vacation

Cars and spaceships

Consider how very disparate things may have something in common. By analogous thinking you may be able to create mental links between what you know and something entirely new.

chapter 4

Authority

" **I**NFORMATION RESOURCES REFLECT THEIR CREATORS' EXPERTISE AND CREDIBIL-
ity, and are evaluated based on the information need and the context in which
the information will be used. Authority is constructed in that various communities may recognize different types of authority. It is contextual in that the
information need may help to determine the level of authority required."[1]
Students often have trouble understanding authority as a concept —a threshold
concept, if you will. Students are not used to considering what makes a person an
authority on a subject. To young people, everyone who is older and who has more life
experience appears to be an authority. Until they have some experience of their own,
students have few internal tools to help them decide whether someone is qualified to
speak on a subject. Information literacy instruction can offer some valuable clues about
determining authority and explaining why it is important. Once students understand
what "authority" is and how to determine who has it, they can master the concept
and move across the threshold. They need practice in identifying credentials and the
relative strength of those credentials as compared to the reliability of the information
received. They need to understand the different types of credentials and how each type
is applicable when addressing information needs.

WHAT IS AUTHORITY?

The *Merriam-Webster Dictionary* defines authority as

1. A citation (as from a book or file) used in defense or support : the
   source from which the citation is drawn; a conclusive statement or

    set of statements (as an official decision of a court) : a decision taken as a precedent : testimony; an individual cited or appealed to as an expert

2. Power to influence or command thought, opinion, or behavior; freedom granted by one in authority : right
3. Persons in command; specifically, government; a governmental agency or corporation to administer a revenue-producing public enterprise : [e.g.,] the transit authority
4. Grounds, warrant : [someone] had excellent authority for believing the claim; convincing force: [someone] lent authority to the performance (www.merriam-webster.com/dictionary/authority)

The word *authority* springs from the word *author.* Authors are seen as people who have expert knowledge of a topic and have written about it. The first definitions for *authority* apply directly to this sense of the word. If you cite a written source, you cite an authority, based on the assumption that the person who wrote the book knows what he is talking about. The written or oral conclusion of a court is also assumed to have been produced by someone knowledgeable in the field under consideration and is, therefore, an authority. A situation or decision may also constitute a kind of authority (termed a *precedent*) when it is used to support a subsequent, similar situation. Finally an individual who is "cited or appealed to as an expert" is considered an authority.

The second definition for the word *authority* also applies to information literacy, but in a more subtle way. Someone in authority has the right to "command thought, opinion, or behavior" because she is in a position of power. The CEO of a corporation, for example, has the authority to direct the work of that company. She can set the rules and suspend those rules. The CEO can make decisions for the entire company. She can allow workers to dress casually on Fridays or expect them to work overtime. She can grant days off or offer professional education programs. The CEO has administrative authority. Of course, the CEO usually gets to the top because she is well educated and well informed and has the necessary experience to make decisions that make the company successful, so she may also have subject-related authority.

According to the third definition, people give authority to someone—that is, they allow someone to do something—usually because the person has extensive training, education, experience, and a track record for providing reliable information and can be entrusted to use the authority to do a job. Members of Congress have the authority to make laws because the voters in their districts elected them to do so. Voters assume that those they elect to Congress are well informed and well educated. Voters give their elected officials the authority to make laws.

The last definition points to the source of a decision or conclusion. The authority in the background is the cause of the conclusion. If you "have something on good authority," you have consulted an accurate, reliable source. If an action is done with strength and confidence (with authority), people feel that the action is accurate and reliable—whether it is or is not is another matter.

Types of Authority

As with anything else, there is a range of authority. Anyone who knows more than you do about something could be an authority of sorts. This assumption creates something of a problem for someone with no knowledge at all in a particular area. It's hard to know whether the information you are getting is accurate and reliable if you don't know anything about the subject. Depending on what you want to know and how important it is to get in-depth information, you might look for someone who claims to be an authority on the topic. The problem is that someone can claim to be an authority, even if he is not. This difficulty is especially true in the world of online information. It takes a bit of detective work to find out how much authority someone really has. In the online world, this discovery can require more than a little detective work because stating one's credentials is not required.

In the world of information, we often depend on people we trust to confirm that someone is an authority, and we refer to the same person those people refer to. In daily life, the person your friends think is a good tax accountant is probably someone you can trust to be a good tax accountant. You base your opinion on the opinion of others you trust. In the literature of a subject area, writers and researchers select a variety of earlier writers and researchers to support the points they are trying to make. The earlier authors are cited as authorities on the subject. The more often an author is cited in the literature on a subject, the more basis there is to assume that she is an authority on that subject.

Sometimes we look for authority conferred on someone by the nature of his job. For example, the surgeon general of the United States is appointed the top medical authority in the country. In becoming surgeon general the candidate demonstrates that he has a deep knowledge of medicine. The candidate has probably done much research, much writing, and much teaching to get to the point where he can be considered for the post of surgeon general. The president and Congress have looked over the candidate's credentials and found that they show the applicant to be qualified. If the president and Congress confer the title of surgeon general on someone, they are confident that this person is an authority in the field of medicine. By extension we can also infer the same.

Sometimes authority comes from the organization rather than from the individual. We talk about the authority of "the church" or "the government." Although the church and the government are made up of individuals, it is the organization that carries the authority for all those associated with it. Patrick Wilson writes, "The point of a formal organization is to give authority to offices that does not depend exclusively on the characteristics of the individuals who fill them."[2] Authority is conferred on individuals who represent an institution because people trust that the institution will not allow a non-authority to speak for it.

Credentials That Confer Authority

Who is an authority? How do you know? What is it that makes a person an authority? Are there different levels of authority? Are there different standards of authority for different subjects? How does one get to be an authority on a subject? How much authority do you need? Students ask all these questions. Most students have a basic understanding of expertise, but they do not know how that expertise translates into authority, and they often don't understand how that authority relates to the selection of sources of information.

When you have a question, you want to find an answer that is both accurate and reliable. One way to ensure that the information you select is accurate and reliable is to get that information from someone who is an authority on that subject. But what makes a person an authority? The following criteria come to mind:

- *Education or training:* Someone who has had a lot of education in the field in question is likely to know a lot about the subject. She has had the time to study both the general and the specific aspects of the subject. She has taken many classes and done lots of homework related to the subject.
- *Expertise:* Someone with expertise has had a lot of practice doing what he does. A certain amount of authority comes with expertise.
- *Experience:* Someone with experience is likely to have practical knowledge about the subject. She may have applied academic or other training to real-life situations and thus become an authority.
- *Recognition:* Someone may become a "recognized authority" because of awards won, titles conferred, research completed, and so on.
- *Charisma:* Someone may be so convincing that people simply want to believe what that person tells them.
- *Institutional authority:* Some people gain authority from the institution they work for. The reputation of the institution confers some authority on the individuals who belong to that institution.

Someone can have many years of *education* about bicycles. An engineer who designs bicycles might have studied the shape and mechanical workings of the bicycle, the physics of how the bicycle operates, the kinesiology of the rider, the logistics of creating bike lanes and bike paths, the best surfaces for different kinds of tires, the safety issues, and so on. In-depth education and training can help make a person an authority or expert on a subject.

Expertise is often the only credential people use to decide whether someone has authority. But is expertise really enough? How much knowledge about something is enough to make someone an expert? K. Anders Ericsson and colleagues, in studying musicians, determined that "becoming an expert required an average of 10,000 hours of focused practice."[3] The best musicians accumulated many hours of practice, which helped make them expert musicians. Baseball players become expert hitters by hitting the baseball over and over again. Just because someone becomes an expert in a field does not necessarily make that person an authority, but those of us outside the field tend to assume that many hours of practice give someone a certain authority on a subject.

One way to gain authority, then, is to become an expert. The way to become an expert is to practice your business for ten thousand hours or more. Presumably spending that much time practicing will make you pretty good at what you do, whether that is playing the violin or repairing cars. We assume that anyone who has done something long enough will gain some authority on that subject. (It might be wise, though, to consider whether the coach or the trainer could be the real authority behind the expert.)

The perceived authority of an expert may vary depending on the person seeking the information. For example, when a physicist is seeking an authority on the physics of bike riding, he may turn to another physicist because that person "speaks" physics. He understands the education and training that another physicist has. He has the means to find out what research and writing the authority has done concerning bike riding. On the other hand, when a bike racer is seeking an authority on bike racing, she may tend to turn to another bike racer, rather than to a physicist.

Depending on the level of information needed, the level of expertise required could also change. For example, if you wanted to know how much to inflate the tires on your new bike, you could find the answer in a number of places: a store that sells bikes like yours, a website about bikes and tires, a friend who rides a bike, and so on. If you wanted to know how much to inflate your tires to gain optimal performance and wear because your bike messenger service has only a small budget for tire replacement, you might turn to authorities with expertise aligned to your specific need: the tire manufacturer, a transportation expert, or a physicist, for example.

For information about bike helmets, you could use a source such as *Consumer Reports*. You could use information from a Consumer Product Safety Commission report. You could use information from a professional bike racing website. For information about keeping your six-year-old safe on her first bike, you might look at the preceding sources or you might look for the specific safety features and crash test results published in a government report or academic journal. Or you might simply ask your neighbor whose children are a little older than yours.

Someone with *experience* could be an authority. For example, we could assume that Chris Froome, a winner of the Tour de France bike race, probably knows a great deal about the parts of the bicycle and what makes it operate. He probably knows a good deal about how to operate the bike in different conditions of weather and terrain and about what kind of tire to use for each. He will know about bike paths and bike lanes. He will know what is required by the human body to operate the bicycle. He will know what he needs to do to operate the bike safely. J. K. Rowling has a lot of experience writing successful books. She knows how to tell a story, create characters, use language and imagination, and so on. Her experience with writing is part of what might make her an authority about writing.

Someone may have the *recognition* of people who consider him an authority. By virtue of the work this person has done in the past, some followers have recognized him as an authority. Based on the established recognition of an authority by a group of followers, others may choose to accept the beliefs of the followers. (Bill tells Frank that Joe is an expert trumpet player. Frank accepts that Joe is an expert trumpet player based on what Bill tells him.) This acceptance confers authority based on association rather than on direct knowledge.

A *charismatic* authority is someone whose message is so compelling that people consider it to be true and accurate. This belief might be based only on the convincing nature of the delivery of the message, or it might be because the message is compelling, or it might be that the message answers a vital question for the listener. For one reason or another, people may want to believe a charismatic message. They may suspend other means of evaluating authority and simply confer authority based on the persona of the individual. In some cases charisma is coupled with other attributes that make the assumption of authority a reasonable conclusion. In other cases it can lead to disaster.

In the search for information, the expertise of the person offering the information is important. Ideally an authority will have both experience and education. The best authorities have both theoretical and practical knowledge of their subject. They have a track record of providing accurate and reliable information.

WHAT IS A CREDENTIAL?

What is it that convinces people that someone is an authority? People often look for credentials which help show that a person has education, expertise, or experience in some area. Credentials can vary in scope. Street credentials, for example, simply amount to an expressed general feeling about someone. In filmmaking, for example, someone with "street cred" is accepted by the people who have seen her work and consider it good. Someone who creates one or more films that people enjoy gains street cred. A weather forecaster who accurately predicts the weather for the coming week also has a certain amount of street cred, and people will turn to that forecaster when they want to know what the weather is going to be like. So the person who has a track record for successful movie making or weather forecasting has credentials based on nothing more than the past experience of the public.

Sometimes experience alone is enough to prove one's credibility (believability). When looking for a car mechanic, one would hope to find someone who has experience in car repair. Anyone can hang up a sign offering car repair services, but it is likely that an individual with some years of experience will have a better chance of doing the repair correctly and efficiently. Credibility for the mechanic can be based on years of experience in car repair. This *informal credential* can be gained by almost anyone if he is right often enough.

There are other means of determining how well a car repair might be done. For example, auto mechanics are often certified (given a diploma or certificate) to show that they have completed a course of training in repairing cars. This certificate or diploma is a *formal credential* that indicates a certain level of expertise in the field. Some manufacturers require ongoing training in the repair of their product. So the auto mechanic who earns a diploma from a trade school has a credential. In addition, a mechanic may be required by a specific car company to get ongoing training in order to work on specific cars. The additional training is also a credential the auto mechanic can offer to those seeking car repairs. A car mechanic may gain some credibility by working for a particular car company. If the company is known for mechanical excellence, the mechanic gains a *credential by association*—people will assume that a company known for mechanical excellence will hire only expert mechanics. Going back to the television weather forecaster, that person is likely a meteorologist. It is likely that she has an advanced degree in meteorology from a university. This formal credential conveys authority to the person who earns it.

Outside agencies often rate the success of products. *Consumer Reports,* for example, has writers who review current products and report to readers about those products. The reviewers who write for this well-respected publication gain authority simply by working for a well-regarded publication. People who read their reviews assume that the reviewers are authorities on the products they write about. Their expertise is assumed not just from the content of the reviews they write but also from the reputation of the publication they work for. Their credential in this case comes by association with an authoritative publication.

People with experience and training in a field will look for specific credentials. A film student trying to identify an authority on film might look for someone with an advanced degree in higher education or awards won for filmmaking, or both. A professor of film studies trying to identify an authority on film might look for someone with an advanced degree in higher education, a record of receiving funding for research, and a history of winning prizes, along with recommendations from others working in the same field or the reputation of the institution for whom the authority works. As the expertise of the researcher increases, the specificity of the credentials required becomes much more exacting.

The difficulty is that it takes time and effort to determine whether someone has authority of the type and level needed. Authority is often based on assumptions. If those assumptions are faulty, the authority relied upon may be faulty. If the authority is faulty, the information you get may be incomplete, inaccurate, or just plain wrong. If we are seeking information about good mechanics and consult only people who drive Toyotas, we don't get a very rounded picture of car repair possibilities, and we could easily obtain information that does not apply to Fords or Mazdas.

In general, the nature of the need to know will dictate the level of expertise or authority that is acceptable. Teachers of information literacy can encourage students to practice their critical thinking skills by creating exercises that ask students to identify their assumptions about authority, question those assumptions, and seek information that will support or refute those assumptions.

How does this search for authority and credentials translate into information literacy? The following exercises offer some practical examples.

NOTES

1. Association of College and Research Libraries, *Framework for Information Literacy for Higher Education* (Chicago: American Library Association, 2015), www.ala.org/acrl/standards/ilframework.

2. Patrick Wilson, *Second-Hand Knowledge: An Inquiry into Cognitive Authority* (Westport, CT: Greenwood, 1983), 81.

3. K. Anders Ericsson, Ralf Th. Krampe, and Clemens Tesch-Romer, "The Role of Deliberate Practice in the Acquisition of Expert Performance," *Psychological Review* 100, no. 3 (1993): 363–406.

EXERCISE 22

Hurricane Information

LEARNING OUTCOMES

- Students will learn that different information needs may require different levels of expertise.
- Students will learn that different levels of authority are acceptable in the context of the information need.
- Students will learn that different sources of expertise may be needed for different types of information needs.

The instructor should discuss with students the concept of authority and how it might differ from one situation to another. Students should work in small groups to identify a specific authority who could provide the information needed for each of the following scenarios. The working groups should report their results to the class and elaborate on the authorities selected.

INSTRUCTIONS

In small groups discuss and record your answers to the following question:

What authority would be good enough to provide information in each of the following scenarios? Why?

- You are doing a report on hurricanes for a high school project.
- You just moved to Rhode Island. You want to know your risk of experiencing a hurricane and how much hurricane insurance you will need.
- You live in Bermuda and want to be prepared for the next hurricane that comes along.
- A hurricane is bearing down and a direct hit is expected in your neighborhood in coastal North Carolina.

Are You an Authority?

LEARNING OUTCOMES

- Students will learn that authority is relative to the information need and to the level of knowledge of the audience.
- Students will learn that in some cases they can be authorities.

The instructor may conduct this exercise as a class or in small groups.

INSTRUCTIONS

Complete the following steps:

Step 1. Write down some traits (e.g., education) that would allow you to identify an authority on a subject.

Step 2. Discuss authority—What is it? Who has it? How do you know? Write some of your ideas on a whiteboard or flip chart.

Step 3. Identify an area that you know something about and write it down (e.g., reading, riding a bicycle, bowling, etc.).

Step 4. Identify an audience for whom you would be an "authority" in the area you identified (first graders, people learning to ride bikes, people learning to read, non-bowlers, etc.—in essence, those who have less experience than you do).

Step 5. Identify an audience for whom you would *not* be an "authority" (people with higher degrees in the field, Lance Armstrong, reading teachers, bowling league champions, etc.).

Step 6. Summarize what you have learned about authority and who can be one. Write those ideas on a whiteboard or flip chart.

EXERCISE 24

Political Pundits

Students hear a lot about political candidates but often know nothing about those candidates' credentials.

LEARNING OUTCOMES

- Students will learn about sources for information about the credentials of political candidates.
- Students will learn to compare and contrast authorities that provide credentials of political candidates.

The instructor should provide a list of political candidates for whom information is readily available (e.g., candidates for president of the United States). The instructor may want to provide links to the sources needed for each part of the exercise rather than have students spend time trying to locate appropriate sites.

INSTRUCTIONS

Record the following information from the websites indicated:

List the credentials of each candidate, using the candidate's website (e.g., education, political experience, leadership experience, etc.).

Find an outside source of biographical information about each candidate. Note any discrepancies or omissions between this source and the previous source.

Find information from an organization that does *not* support the candidate in question (e.g., a Republican website giving information about a Democrat and vice versa).

Write down everything you consider to be a credential for each candidate.

Based on the information gathered, answer the following questions:

What credentials would make you think that the candidate is an authority?

Are there differences in what is reported in different sources?

Are any biases apparent in what is reported?

Are the credentials found sufficient to allow you to determine whether the candidate is qualified to run for the office of president of the United States?

Thinking Critically about Authority

LEARNING OUTCOMES

- Students will learn that people of equal authority may not agree.

Students may work in small groups, as a class, or individually. This exercise can be done in class or as a homework assignment. The instructor should find two experts who disagree or come to different conclusions about the same topic (the topic should be a current controversy the students can relate to, such as media bias, gun control, immigration, smoking, etc.). The instructor should provide an article by each author on the subject. If the exercise is to be done in class, the articles should be given to students ahead of time so they can read the material before class.

INSTRUCTIONS

Summarize the main points of each article, including the conclusion reached, and answer the following questions:

Based on the following, what is the authority of each author?
- Education
- Experience
- Publication record
- Most recent publication on the topic in question
- Years in the field

Author of article 1:
Author of article 2:

What are the main points supporting each argument, and what conclusion was reached?
Article 1:
Article 2:

In what type of publication does the article appear (scholarly journal, magazine, trade publication)?
Article 1:
Article 2:

From what type of institution did the authors receive their training?
Article 1:
Article 2:

At what type of institution do the authors work?
>   Article 1:
>   Article 2:

Does each expert provide data on the topic? Where did the data come from? How were the data collected?
>   Article 1:
>   Article 2:

What are some possible reasons that people with equal authority on a subject might come to different conclusions?

Psychological studies show that people tend to seek out information that agrees with what they already believe. Can this phenomenon have an effect on the results of a study? Did it have an effect on the two articles in question? (*Hint:* Compare the bibliographies.)
>   Article 1:
>   Article 2:

What are some ways you might be able to determine which author has more authority (e.g., seek out more information from other experts and see which conclusion has more support, wait for further studies to be done, unable to determine ever)?

Authority and Turmeric

LEARNING OUTCOMES

- Students will learn the time-consuming nature of authority checking.
- Students will learn the importance of using authoritative sources.
- Students will learn that information from often-used sources is not always based on authoritative information.

In the context of wanting to know what turmeric is, how it is used, and what medical properties it might have, a student might consult a source like *Wikipedia*. The instructor should use as much or as little of the detail outlined in the exercise as needed for students to understand the time-consuming and sometimes complex process of establishing authority.

INSTRUCTIONS

Go to *Wikipedia*, look up the term "turmeric," and answer the following questions:

What are the parts of the entry for "turmeric"?

At Wikipedia, the reader will find a pronunciation, a definition, and a description of the plant as well as a picture of the plant in flower. Botanical information, including the plant's Latin name, is given. The article tells where the plant grows and under what conditions. The article then gives a history of the plant and what it has been used for. This discussion is followed by an explanation of the pronunciation, a botanical description, the biochemical composition, uses for the plant—culinary, folk medicine and traditional uses, preliminary medical research, use as a dye, known drawbacks to its use, use in ceremonies and myths—and a "See also" list. Finally, a References list cites the sources of the information.

Who is the author of the article?

The author(s) of the article are not named. That means it is not possible to determine the authority of the person or persons who pulled all the information together and created the article on turmeric.

What else in the article might help determine whether the information is authoritative?

The references cited offer the names of many who may be experts in the field. Determining the status of the authors of the references would go a long way toward reassuring the reader that the information is accurate and reliable. It is, however, one step removed from the authority of the author of the article. That may or may not matter, depending on the need for the information.

Are the references cited authoritative?

If more authoritative or specific information is needed, the student can follow up on the articles listed in the References. For example, if the focus of the investigation is medical uses of turmeric, the student would turn to the articles cited in the "Preliminary medical research" section of the Wikipedia article.

Look at the article titled "Herbs at a Glance" cited in the References list.

Who is the author of this article?
Who is the publisher or sponsor of this article?

This document is a general fact sheet published by the National Institutes of Health. This fact sheet gives much of the same general information found at the Wikipedia site. It also includes a section titled "What the Science Says" and a section called "Side Effects and Cautions." No author is cited for this fact sheet, so again, it is necessary to look at the authors of the articles listed in the Key References section of the fact sheet.

Look at the references cited in the NIH fact sheet. Go to the first website listed (Turmeric. Natural Medicines Comprehensive Database Web site. Accessed at www .naturaldatabase.com on July 22, 2009).

Who is the author or sponsor of the website?
Does this website support the information in the NIH fact sheet?
How long ago was the website updated?
What is the age of the information at the website?

In examining the first website, we find information about its purpose and history along with a long list of contributors with medical credentials. Pharmacists, medical doctors, and other health professionals created the database. It appears to be updated daily. Despite its status as a dot-com site, it appears to be compiled by people who are authorities in the medical field and who have an interest in natural medicines. The NIH fact sheet cites it. Even though we don't know specifically who wrote the article, it seems like a good bet that the information is accurate and reliable.

Follow the same procedure for the other website shown in the NIH fact sheet's Key References list: Turmeric (*Curcuma longa* Linn.) and curcumin. Natural Standard Database Web site. Accessed at www.naturalstandard.com on July 22, 2009.

> Who is the author or sponsor of the website?
> Does this website support the information in the NIH fact sheet?
> How long ago was the website updated?
> What is the age of the information at the website?

Now look at the third item in the NIH fact sheet's Key References list: Turmeric root. In: Blumenthal M, Goldberg A, Brinckman J, eds. *Herbal Medicine: Expanded Commission E Monographs*. Newton, MA: Lippincott Williams & Wilkins; 2000: 379–384.

> Who is the author of the herbal medicine book?
> Who is the author of the article on turmeric?
> Does the information cited support the information on the NIH fact sheet?
> Does the information cited support the information on the *Wikipedia* site?
> Is the information current?

> *The third citation in the NIH fact sheet's Key References list comes from a textbook published by a reputable medical publisher. The information provided is not current, according to the citation (the textbook was published in 2000). In examining the textbook, we find that it is an edited encyclopedia of sorts, listing herbal medicines by name in alphabetical order. The article on turmeric is three pages long. Once again, the reader must rely on the reputation of the editors as the authorship of the specific article is unknown. The editors are all researchers with multiple publications concerning herbal medicine.*

Go back to the original *Wikipedia* article's References list. Go to the website for the article titled "Turmeric" published by the American Cancer Society.

> Does this website support the authority of the *Wikipedia* entry on turmeric?
> Who wrote the information?
> How old is the information?

> *This link from the* Wikipedia *article takes the reader to the American Cancer Society website's section on complementary and alternative medicine. The information given is about cancer treatments using herbal medicines and general information about using dietary supplements. This information is very general. It is not specific to turmeric. The advice given is to consult with a doctor before taking any medication. No*

specific author is listed. The information was last reviewed and updated in March 2015.

Go back to the References list at the *Wikipedia* article. Go to the website for the following article: *Ragasa C, Laguardia M, Rideout J (2005). "Antimicrobial sesquiterpenoids and diarylheptanoid from Curcuma domestica."*

Does this website support the authority of the *Wikipedia* entry on turmeric?
Who wrote the information?
How old is the information?

This article from the Wikipedia References list is a scholarly refereed journal article from a Malaysian UNESCO publication called ACGC (Asian Coordinating Group for Chemistry) Chemical Research Communications. The article was published in 2005 and therefore is not current. The credentials of the authors are not given, but judging from the very specific content of the article, they appear to be experts in the field of chemistry as applied to herbal medicine.

Go back to the References list at the *Wikipedia* article. Go to the website for the article titled "Clinical trials on turmeric" published by the National Institutes of Health.

Does this website support the authority of the *Wikipedia* entry on turmeric?
Who wrote the information?
How old is the information?

This article is from a U.S. government website concerning clinical trials for various medicines. The website lists many clinical trials concerning turmeric. Of those trials, less than half have been completed. Only two trials are listed as having results. The two studies were very small so their results would not be generalized to the larger population. The authors were non-U.S. medical professionals.

Go back to the References list at the *Wikipedia* article. Go to the website for the article by Mishra and Palanivelu titled *"The effect of curcumin (turmeric) on Alzheimer's disease: An overview."*

Does this website support the authority of the *Wikipedia* entry on turmeric?

Who wrote the information?
How old is the information?

> *The article appears in the refereed journal* Annals of Indian Academy of Neurology. *At last we find an article with a named author! Shrikant Mishra works in the Department of Neurology at the VA/USC in Sepulveda, California. Kalpana Palanivelu has written many articles in this and other health-related areas.*

Go back to the References list at the *Wikipedia* article. Go to the website for the article by Boaz and others titled "*Functional foods in the treatment of type 2 diabetes: olive leaf extract, turmeric and fenugreek, a qualitative review.*"

Does this website support the authority of the *Wikipedia* entry on turmeric?
Who wrote the information?
How old is the information?

> *This article was published in* Functional Foods in Health and Disease *in 2011. The authors work in various units of the Wolfson Medical Center and in the Department of Nutrition at Ariel University Center, both in Israel. One page of the ten-page paper contains information about the use of turmeric in the treatment of diabetes.*

Does anything you have read or examined from the References list at the *Wikipedia* site for "turmeric" state that turmeric is conclusively an effective treatment for any disease?

> *In general, all the articles cited indicate that there is not enough evidence to support the claim that turmeric (or its active ingredient curcumin) is an effective treatment for any disease. One study indicated that curcumin was "possibly effective" in treating osteoarthritis, providing as much relief as ibuprofen. A serious two hours of follow-up research from the* Wikipedia *article about turmeric, linking to the referenced articles, resulted in minimal information about the authority of those providing the backup information. Students who do not have a serious research interest in turmeric would probably not spend the time needed to follow up on the authority of the* Wikipedia *page.*

EXERCISE 27

Authority in the Workplace

This exercise will encourage students to think about what people in real-life situations look for in terms of authority.

LEARNING OUTCOMES

- Students will learn to recognize the need for authority in real-life situations.
- Students will articulate what kinds of authority they would look for in a real-life situation.

This exercise can be done individually, but students would benefit from group discussion at the end and guidance from the instructor if necessary. The instructor should allow students time to answer the question on paper and then have the entire group discuss their ideas.

INSTRUCTIONS

Corporations and businesses, especially large ones, rely on the authority of specialists who work for the company. The CEO will rely on the authority of a legal advisor, a financial advisor, a marketing advisor, a production advisor, and so on. The CEO is not expected to know everything.

Imagine you are the CEO of a large company that makes widgets. You are interviewing candidates for the job of chief financial officer for your company. List credentials (e.g., education, experience, training, career development learning opportunities like workshops, etc.) that you would look for in each résumé that might show you that the candidates are authorities in the field.

1.

2.

3.

4.

chapter 5

Information Creation as a Process

" **I**NFORMATION IN ANY FORMAT IS PRODUCED TO CONVEY A MESSAGE AND IS shared via a selected delivery method. The iterative processes of researching, creating, revising, and disseminating information vary, and the resulting product reflects these differences."[1] Information is produced to convey a message. Most of the time that message is produced intentionally. There are many different kinds of messages. We are bombarded by messages all day, every day. By deconstructing some of the types of messages we receive, we may understand how information is created and conveyed, what that means with regard to our consumption of that information, and, more important, how we can teach students to be aware of the processes involved in the creation of information.

SHORT FORMATS

Some messages are quite short. These short messages are created to link a word or a few words with a person, place, company, or idea. For example, during political campaigns of the past, people wore a lapel pin with the name of the candidate they supported on it. The message told anyone who read it something about the person wearing the pin. The pin might identify the political party the wearer supported as well as the candidate supported. It might say something about the worldview of the wearer (liberal, conservative, radical). It might convey that the wearer was a member of an in-group who knew the candidate well enough to call him by his first name. The political lapel pin was worn to convey one or more messages. The pin certainly conveyed the name of the candidate and, when seen often, created name recognition for the candidate. The message was short. The purpose of the message was to generate one or more reactions based on the viewer's political leanings and knowledge.

Another kind of short message is a logo or a motto. Nike Inc. uses the same logo, a simple checkmark (the "swoosh"), on all its products. The purpose of the logo is to get people to associate the symbol with the brand. The logo allows people to identify products made by Nike without needing to see the name. If the logo is successful, it will cause people to think of Nike every time they see a checkmark of any kind. (Repetition helps to move information in the brain to long-term memory where automated processes reside. Recognition of a logo associated with a product will eventually become automatic. See chapter 8.) The information or message conveyed by the logo is very limited. The idea is to cause the viewer to remember the product or company the logo stands for.

The same is true for a motto. A motto is a statement of belief or expectation. Every state in the United States has a motto. The Girl Scouts have a motto. Many companies have mottoes. IBM uses a very short message as its motto to remind employees about what the company feels is important and to tell the public something about the company. The IBM motto is Think. This motto was coined by Thomas J. Watson while he worked for the National Cash Register Company in 1911.[2] In 1914, when Watson moved to the company that was to become IBM, he brought the motto with him. He felt the single word conveyed to employees and to the public that IBM employees were expected to consider every aspect of a problem. Further, it conveyed to the public that employees of IBM *would* consider every aspect of a problem. They would use their brains to find the best solutions. This motto was placed on signs in IBM buildings and conference rooms and was widely used in advertising about IBM. Over time, the motto Think has become routinely linked to IBM by the public. When people hear the word "think," it may bring IBM to mind.

Some other brief messages are collectively called *branding*. A company, a college, an organization, a political party will choose a symbol or a word, a uniform color, a standardized message that will be used in every way possible to link that symbol or word with the company, college, organization, or political party. The message is very brief and works largely by association rather than by conveying information in the context of the message.

In the age of electronics, a common form of short message is a "tweet." This communication is sent through an electronic messaging company called Twitter. The company makes it possible for a client to send short messages (only 140 characters or less) to people who are interested in what the client has to say. Because the messages are sent electronically, they are meant only for the segment of the population that can receive electronic messages. Further, out of the segment of the population that can receive electronic messages, only those who agree to receive messages from particular people will receive them. (These people are called followers.) President Barack Obama "tweets" to those people who can receive electronic messages and who have agreed to receive those messages from him. The purpose of a tweet is to share a short message with a select group of people. It allows news to be conveyed quickly but does not allow for much detail.

Other forms of short messages include colors, banners, postcards, and personal appearance (uniforms, jewelry, hair style and color, etc.). The color pink has become associated with the fight against breast cancer. The color yellow is associated with bringing service men and women home from dangerous deployments. Banners can convey information about events—time, place, date. Postcards can provide a limited amount of information for a number of purposes. The message might be personal, informational, or promotional. It might be verbal or visual or both. These short messages are created and disseminated in specific ways for specific purposes. They often work by association, as the information they can contain is limited. They are often used when time and space are limited.

LONG FORMATS

Often we need to deliver more information than can be contained in a motto or a tweet. When a larger amount of information needs to be conveyed, the format for delivering that information expands. The length of the message affects the medium used to deliver the message. A lapel button is great for delivering a one-word message. A tweet is a good way to deliver a thought or to ask a quick question. However, when there is more information to convey, other methods work better.

When shopping for a new car, one must consider many things—make and model, cost, mileage, options, service, and so on. Car companies often combine information about their products in one place, so the car-buying public can get answers to questions easily. One example is a brochure from a car company. The brochure might show a picture of the vehicle, give the estimated miles per gallon, list the features that are standard and those that are optional, show the colors available, give the phone number and hours of the dealership and the service department, and so on. Today, this brochure might be printed or available electronically. This kind of information is designed to help car manufacturers sell cars. These formats are chosen because they help people see the product and get at least a general idea about the product specifics the manufacturer wants to emphasize. This kind of information is not meant to be comprehensive. It is a convenience for customers, and it allows car manufacturers to highlight particular aspects of their products. If this information were sent out on Twitter, many, many messages would be required to convey it all.

A second long message format is a blog. A blog is "a discussion or informational site published on the World Wide Web consisting of discrete entries ('posts') typically displayed in reverse chronological order (the most recent post appears first)."[3] Most blogs are about specific subjects. Sometimes one person writes the blog alone, and other times a group of people are involved. The author may be an expert on a topic or not. Subjects covered range from personal diaries to politics to quantum mechanics. Most blogs allow readers to comment, making the communication somewhat interactive. The information conveyed is from both the author and the readers. The blog posting usually conveys an essay-length message. The information may be based on research or may be based entirely on opinion. Because software has been designed to assist in the creation of blogs, bloggers do not need any advanced technical or computer skills to create their blogs, making this method of conveying information available to anyone with an interest and an Internet connection. Most blogs are freely available on the Internet.

A newspaper is another long format designed to provide the current news. A newspaper may contain any number of articles written by any number of journalists on any topic. The publishers or producers of newspapers may create a general source of information or one that specializes in the news of a particular geographic location, political party, or subject category. They will hire reporters and editors to create the stories. The purpose for the newspaper is to gather different stories written by different people and bundle them together so that readers have a broad sense of current events in many categories. Newspapers were traditionally printed on paper but have largely moved to electronic format. Traditionally newspapers were only minimally interactive. Journalists are taught to report their stories to answer the questions *who, what, where, when,* and *why.* For some sources, like newspapers, the basic information is all that is required. For other sources, like news magazines, stories tend to be longer, so more detail can be supplied.

Newspapers and magazines report news and other information. An organization usually produces the information for consumption by the public or by a specific interest group. The organization hires people to do the writing, gathers the writing for dissemination on a schedule, organizes and edits the information according to rules the organization has set, and releases the information to the public. This process means that those who control the organization control the content as well. They choose what to publish, they set guidelines about content and style, and they may target specific points of view or specific subjects. Those who control these publications act as gatekeepers. They filter and select information for dissemination. This type of information may be published in paper or electronic format. Financial support comes from individual purchase of each publication, from advertising, or from both.

Scholarly journals are collections of articles written by experts in their fields. Journals usually target a specific discipline or subdiscipline and publish only articles related to that area of study. Scholarly journals are usually peer-reviewed, meaning that other experts in the field review the content of each article to determine whether it is worthy of publication. Reviewers consider such questions as, Is it well written? and Does it add new information to the field? The peer reviewer usually does not know whose article she is reading in order to keep the process focused on the content rather than on any personal feelings about the author. Scholarly journals may be published in paper format, but now they are published more commonly in both paper and online formats and sometimes only in online format. Publishers of scholarly journals are a mix of commercial publishers, associations, and organizations. In most cases the publishers act as gatekeepers. The editors decide what will be published. The publishers often require the authors to sign over their copyright. This system allows the publisher to control the information and to charge whatever amount the market will bear to sell the information to scholars, researchers, and academics. In return the publishers provide the peer review, the copyediting, and the platform for the author. Support for the publication comes from paid subscriptions and, in some cases, advertising.

The cost of scholarly journals has skyrocketed during the past twenty years and is now prohibitive for many researchers and their institutions. This high cost limits access to scholarly information to those who can afford to pay for it, which has led to a new movement called the open access movement. The members of this movement create scholarly publications for which the author keeps the copyright and pays a fee to cover the costs of publication. The open access model makes research findings available to more people because publications are essentially free to the reader. Many government agencies are now requiring that information produced with funding from a government research grant must be made available to the public. Open access journals are most often published in electronic format.

Books are a centuries-old format for providing in-depth information. Books can be fiction or nonfiction. They can be of any size and covering. They can be paperback or hardcover. They can be short or long. They can contain text only, pictures only, or a combination of words and pictures, graphs, maps, and other non-text materials. Until recently books were produced only in paper format by publishing houses specializing in specific genres or disciplines. Today books are also published in electronic format and are made available by means of various kinds of readers. The traditional publishers are the gatekeepers, deciding what information to publish. Agents for the publishers receive, review, and recommend manuscripts for publication. The publishers provide services such as editing, indexing, and illustrating. The sale of the book offsets the costs associated with its publication.

Today, self-publishing is possible and frequent through the Internet, even for book-length materials. Authors can publish their work without an agent or a commercial publisher. Books can be self-marketed and sold on the Internet as well. With the advent of e-books, self-publishing authors can inexpensively incorporate non-text materials in their book-length works. The content of e-books can be made searchable. The advent of "easy" self-publishing eliminates the gatekeeping aspect of publishing, allowing ideas to be disseminated quickly and without editorial intervention. That said, with self-publishing the author loses the advantages of expertise in layout, copyediting, marketing, and the many other services that commercial publishers offer. When using a self-published book, the reader loses the benefits of quality control offered by the commercial publishers—everything from spell checking to fact checking.

A website is another long format for information. Anyone can create a website on any subject. Websites can be simple or very complex. They can contain volumes of information, nested in subcategories of the home page, or they can be very simple, one-page sites. One does not have to be an expert in any field to author a website, nor does the information need to be accurate, reliable, or unbiased. The format of the website on the Internet allows easy access to information, makes connections between websites easy, and creates the links between sites that create the actual "web of information." The nature of the web makes it imperative that the searcher beware. It is up to the searcher to evaluate information on the open web and to decide whether the information provided is useful. The web allows free and open expression of thought. No one (except in a very few cases) polices the content or controls the quality of the information offered. Some websites are set up so that people who want to view the content must pay a fee. Many websites are supported by advertising added to the site. In some countries the government restricts access to the web or to parts of the web. In most places there is a charge to connect to the web itself. Sometimes that cost is passed on to the user (Internet access in your home), and sometimes the cost is absorbed by the company or institution providing it (the public library).

VISUAL FORMATS

There are many visual means of conveying information. We all know that a picture can tell a story, evoke an emotion, or pose a question. Paintings have conveyed information for centuries. The Pulitzer Prize for Photography archives a large variety of examples of pictures that convey information. Children's picture books can tell stories (convey information) before a child can read. A picture or series of pictures can supply information without words. We have all seen enough short videos on social media to understand that a story can be told without sound, that information can be conveyed silently or with sounds other than words. Pictures can be used in combination with sound or text or both to create a new format. Videos, documentaries, full-length movies, and online games can all convey information in a purely visual or mixed media presentation. Just as with textual information, the amount of visual information being conveyed will often determine and limit the format used. It is important for students to be able to evaluate the information presented in the many visual formats available in the twenty-first century.

Visual images in general seem to be accepted as credible when the same information in print might not be. In addition, when viewing images, people often see only what they expect to see. They often miss or ignore visual information that they are not expecting to see. In the information age, visual information must be evaluated closely, just as other kinds of information are.

A picture can be sent to an electronic device like a phone. The person who receives the picture may receive it on his phone. Depending on the purpose for the picture, the small screen of the telephone may serve well. To see all the nuances and shades in a painting, however, the small-screen device may not fit the bill. A full-length documentary film can also be sent and received with a telephone, but a device with such a small screen may not convey the information to its best advantage. Because many films are produced to deliver their message on a large screen, the visual message they want to convey can be diluted or changed when viewed in some other format. Selecting a type of information and a format to convey that information plays a big part in the message's success or failure.

Numbers are also information, and the format in which those numbers are conveyed is important. Many of the numbers we deal with every day are statistics. They may be presented just as simple numbers or in the shape of bar graphs, pie charts, flow charts, diagrams, schematics, time lines, maps, word clouds, tables, or complex infographics. Numbers can be used in very convincing ways. It is important to remember that there was a process behind the collection of those numbers, and the process is what makes those numbers valid or invalid. It is also possible to skew the meaning of the numbers through format. By presenting visuals that misrepresent the numbers or the differences between numbers, you can create an inaccurate picture that can influence the viewer.

MULTIPLE FORMATS

Often the same information is available in several different formats. A book, for example, could be available in both print and electronic formats. It might be available in electronic format specific to a device like a Kindle or other type of reader. It may be available in MP3 format. It might be available as an audio book, either on CD or in a computer compatible format. There are sometimes differences in what can be seen, depending on the format used. For some types of information, one type of device provides a better platform or screen than another device would. Some devices provide more viewing options than others. It is good to remember that different formats for the same information may not convey exactly the same information and may not convey that information in the same way. The format used to convey information is specific to that information. The format controls, to some extent, the information that can be conveyed.

NOTES

1. Association of College and Research Libraries, *Framework for Information Literacy for Higher Education* (Chicago: American Library Association, 2015), 6, www.ala.org/acrl/standards/ilframework.

2. "Think (IBM)," *Wikipedia*, https://en.wikipedia.org/wiki/Think_%28IBM%29.

3. "Blog," *Wikipedia*, https://en.wikipedia.org/wiki/Blog.

EXERCISE 28

Logos and Mottoes

Create a logo and a motto.

LEARNING OUTCOMES

- Students will understand how a symbol can represent a physical item.
- Students will recognize the connection between a motto and an organization.

The instructor should provide students with a variety of physical items (e.g., a ruler, a pencil, scissors, a coffee mug, etc.) whose producers have a logo. The instructor should also provide a variety of well-known logos. This exercise may be done individually, in small groups, or as a class. For an in-class exercise, after the students have created their own logos, the instructor should reveal the actual logo for the company that produces each physical item. If students are working individually, the instructor should provide the appropriate web address and ask students to discover the logo for the company. For part 2, the instructor should provide students with the names of a variety of businesses and organizations.

INSTRUCTIONS: PART 1

A logo is a symbol. The symbol should represent something about the company that uses it. Create a logo that represents the company that produces the item you received and write an explanation of how that logo relates to or represents the physical item.

Identify as many as of the logos provided by your instructor as you can. Discuss how and why you can identify some logos and not others.

INSTRUCTIONS: PART 2

Create a short motto that sums up the essence of each company or organization provided by your instructor. Find each company's or organization's own motto. Discuss or write a paragraph about how effective each company's or organization's motto is.

EXERCISE 29

Short Communications

LEARNING OUTCOMES

- Students will be able to summarize information.
- Students will understand how much information can be transmitted in a tweet.

The instructor should provide a short article or a short video.

INSTRUCTIONS

Read the article or watch the video provided by your instructor and then create a tweet that sums up the contents. Remember you are limited to 140 characters. As you compose your tweet, include the answers to the following questions:

Who created the article or video?

What is the article or video about?

Why was it created?

Who is the audience?

How long is it?

Is there anything special we should look out for?

What was your reaction?

Write your tweet here _____ and then answer the following questions:

Were you successful in answering all the questions in the 140 characters allowed?

Is there another format that might be better for conveying this amount of information?

Comparing Efficacy and Limits of Brief Information

LEARNING OUTCOMES

- Students will learn to consider the usefulness of short messages.
- Students will learn how to compare methods of conveying short messages.
- Students will learn how to describe the differences between types of short messages and consider how the different formats affect the message itself.

The instructor should provide trademarks that are well known or locally important.

INSTRUCTIONS

Compare a lapel button, a tweet, and a brochure. List the physical differences between the formats and then answer the following questions:

How do these physical differences affect the delivery of the message? (For example, when would the message on the lapel pin be as effective as a tweet? How big an audience would be reached by each type of message?)

How do the physical differences affect the message itself?

In what situation is each type of message most effective?

Consider the trademarks provided by your instructor. Label all the trademarks that you recognize and then answer the following questions:

How many trademarks did you know?

Can very brief messages convey information effectively?

EXERCISE 31

Long Messages

LEARNING OUTCOMES

- Students will learn to examine the differences between information on blogs.
- Students will learn to consider the credentials of the author of the blog.
- Students will learn to consider the accuracy and reliability of information.
- Students will learn to look for possible bias.

The instructor should provide preselected blogs. This exercise can be done individually or in small groups.

INSTRUCTIONS

Find a blog on any topic and answer the following questions:

What is the subject of this blog?

What is the purpose for the blog?

Name the author and list the individual's credentials. Is this person qualified to discuss this topic?

How often does the author add to the blog?

Is the information presented accurate?

Does the information match what you already know or what other experts say?

Does the blog show any possible bias? Does the blog support one side of an argument? Support your opinion with examples.

Find a second blog and answer the following questions:

What is the subject of this blog?

What is the purpose for the blog?

Name the author and list the individual's credentials. Is this person qualified to discuss this topic?

How often does the author add to the blog?

Is the information presented accurate?

Does the information match what you already know or what other experts say?

Does the blog show any possible bias? Does the blog support one side of an argument? Support your opinion with examples.

Compare your answers for the two blogs and discuss the differences.

EXERCISE 32

Nonverbal Messages

LEARNING OUTCOMES

- Students will learn about assumptions that can be made from nonverbal sources.
- Students will learn how assumptions and opinions formed from nonverbal sources can be inaccurate.

The instructor should provide several photos one at a time. The Pulitzer Prize website (www.pulitzer.org/prize-winners-categories) is a good place to locate iconic photos and photos that evoke human emotions. After the students have answered the following questions, the instructor should reveal the description of the event that goes with each picture.

INSTRUCTIONS

Examine each photo provided by your instructor and answer the following questions:

What information do you get from the photo?

Describe the photo. What are the most distinct things in the photo?

Who is in the photo?

What do you think is happening in this photo?

What assumptions did you make to answer the preceding question?

After learning what was happening when the picture was taken, how close was your guess to the real event in the picture?

Did the picture mislead you in any way?

Did you make any assumptions that were actually untrue?

Did you miss any significant details in the photo?

What did you learn about photographs as information?

Format Comparison

LEARNING OUTCOMES

- Students will learn about the format for popular magazines and scholarly journals.
- Students will learn how the two types of publications differ in terms of their business model.
- Students will learn that many of those differences disappear in the electronic versions of the same two publications.

The instructor should provide paper copies of an article from a magazine and an article from a scholarly journal.

INSTRUCTIONS

Compare a magazine article and a scholarly journal article in paper. Compare format differences only and answer the following questions:

What differences do you find between the popular magazine article and the scholarly journal article?

- Size
- Colors used
- Quality of the paper
- Number of articles in an issue
- Length of the articles in an issue
- Amount of advertising in an issue

Now compare two similar articles online.

How many of the format differences are still apparent?

- Size
- Colors used
- Quality of paper
- Number of articles in an issue
- Length of articles in an issue
- Amount of advertising in an issue

The obvious differences between popular magazines and scholarly journals often disappear when those publications appear online. This characteristic makes it important to evaluate the online article to identify what kind of publication it comes from.

Guess the Message

LEARNING OUTCOMES

- Students will learn how visual and aural messages can work together.
- Students will learn how separating the visual and aural messages can change the message.

The instructor should show a short video, keeping the sound off. The instructor should provide a transcript of the video and then show the video a second time with the sound on.

INSTRUCTIONS

Discuss the content of the video and explain how the format of the information (seeing it on video) impacted the message. Then answer the following questions:

What did you learn from the video-only format?

What was the subject of the video?

Did the video tell a story? What was it?

Was the approach to the subject pro or con?

Did the video evoke any emotion?

Read the transcript (the words) of the video and answer the following questions:

What did you learn from the words of the video?

What was the subject?

Did the words tell a story? What was it?

Was the approach pro or con?

Did the words for the video evoke any emotion?

Watch the video again with sound and answer the following questions:

What more did you learn when sound was added to the video?

Did the pictures and the sound together create a different message than either the pictures or the words alone?

Comparing Formats

LEARNING OUTCOME

- Students will learn the differences between the format of informal information such as a blog and the format of more formal information such as a scholarly journal article.

The instructor should provide a blog posting and a scholarly journal article.

INSTRUCTIONS

Compare the blog posting and the scholarly journal article and answer the following questions:

Who is the author of the blog?

Who is the author of the journal article?

What are the credentials of the author of the blog?

What are the credentials of the author of the journal article?

Is the author of the blog an expert on the subject?

Is the author of the journal article an expert on the subject?

How long is the blog posting?

How long is the journal article?

Are there links to other information embedded in the blog posting?

Are there links to other information embedded in the scholarly article?

What kinds of non-text materials are included in the blog post?

What kinds of non-text materials are included in the scholarly article?

From this blog posting, can you find other postings about the same topic or by the same author?

From the scholarly article, can you find other articles about the same topic or by the same author?

Who published the blog?

Who published the journal article?

Is the information found in the blog different in quality from the information found in the journal article? What would you use each type of information for?

Statistics

LEARNING OUTCOMES

- Students will learn how statistics are used to convey information.
- Students will learn how to evaluate statistics for accuracy and reliability.

The instructor should select one or more tables from the *Statistical Abstract of the United States* for students to evaluate. The instructor should also provide students with a report that gives results of a statistical study. Finally, the instructor should give students an article discussing the results of an opinion poll. (The ICPSR—Inter-university Consortium for Political and Social Research—provides some political research data. The General Social Survey at gss.norc.org is a good source for surveys.) Many popular magazines provide summaries of statistical reports.

INSTRUCTIONS

Look at the table provided by your instructor from the *Statistical Abstract of the United States* and answer the following questions:

What is the purpose for this table?

Who created this table?

How big a sample was collected for this table?

What information does this table provide?

Is it necessary to manipulate the numbers in any way to understand the table?

Now consider a statistical report from the General Social Survey.

What is the purpose of the survey? Why were the data collected?

Who created the survey?

Who administered the survey?

When was the survey administered?

Was there a hypothesis to be proved or disproved? If so, what was it?

How big was the sample size?

How were participants selected?

Did the study test for one variable at a time?

Was there a control group?

Was this a double-blind study?

What did the study conclude? Was the hypothesis disproved?

Based on your evaluation, do you think the information provided is accurate and reliable?

What audience is targeted to receive the results of this study?

Finally, read the article from a popular magazine that summarizes the results of a statistical study and answer the following questions:

What is the purpose of the survey? Why were the data collected?

Who created the survey?

Who administered the survey?

When was the survey administered?

Was there a hypothesis to be proved or disproved? If so, what was it?

How big was the sample size?

How were participants selected?

Did the study test for one variable at a time?

Was there a control group?

Was this a double-blind study?

What did the study conclude? Was the hypothesis disproved?

Based on your evaluation, do you think the information provided is accurate and reliable?

What audience is targeted to receive the results of this study?

Compare the presentations of statistical data in the three sources. Discuss the benefits and drawbacks you find in each. Statistics are often used to make an argument for or against something. Knowing how the data were collected can be very important when relying on the conclusions that can be drawn from those data.

Visual Literacy

LEARNING OUTCOMES

- Students will learn to evaluate visual information.
- Students will learn how visual representations can be manipulated to change their meaning.

The instructor should provide two charts containing the same information, each chart constructed on a different scale. The instructor should provide the same information using several other methods—bar graphs, pie charts, infographics, and the like.

INSTRUCTIONS

Compare the charts provided by your instructor and answer the following questions:

How are the two graphs the same?

How are the two graphs different?

Which graph gives a more accurate representation of the information?

How can the scale on a graph affect the conclusions someone might make about the data?

Look at the next representation of the information (e.g., a pie chart).

Does seeing the information in this format change the visual message and the conclusion you might reach?

Look at the infographic provided.

Does seeing the information in this format change the visual message and conclusion you might reach?

EXERCISE 38

Evaluating Pictures

LEARNING OUTCOMES

- Students will learn to apply evaluation criteria to pictures.
- Students will learn to consider what information has been left out of the picture.

The instructor should provide students with two pictures—a Pulitzer Prize winner and an advertisement.

INSTRUCTIONS

Consider the pictures provided by your instructor one at a time and answer the following questions about each:

Who is the audience for this picture? Who is the author trying to reach with this picture?

What is the context for the picture? Are there any background elements that contribute to the overall message?

What is the main focus of the picture? Who or what is pictured?

What is the purpose or goal for the image? Is it advertising? Persuasion?

What is the tone of the picture? Is the tone of the picture serious, lighthearted, playful, sad?

What is the scale of the picture? Are the elements of the picture large or small? Is any element out of scale with the others?

Where are the individual elements placed in the picture—are they centered, offset, scattered?

Is movement implied or depicted in the picture?

Is a clear emotion being depicted?

What colors are used in the picture?

Do the colors used create any human emotion (e.g., warm colors indicate human warmth)?

Is there any text in the picture itself (street signs, building names, etc.)? What information does that add to the picture? (Does it tell you, for example, where the picture was taken, or the time period it was taken in?)

Does the picture have a caption? If so, is the font size unusually large or small, fancy or plain? What does the information in the caption add to the picture's message?

What is your impression of what is going on in the picture?

How do the two pictures differ?

What is the reason for the differences you identify?

chapter 6

Searching as Strategic Exploration

SEARCHING FOR INFORMATION IS OFTEN NONLINEAR AND ITERATIVE, requiring the evaluation of a range of information sources and the mental flexibility to pursue alternate avenues as new understanding develops."[1] We live in an age in which an instant response to any query is the expected norm. Students today have never been without the Google search box. If they want to know something, they Google it, and whatever the search brings back is the answer. Although instant gratification is appealing, the instant answers of Google are sometimes less than adequate and sometimes so overwhelming in quantity that it is impossible to sift out a simple answer to a simple question. Further, there are some instances in which a Google search brings results, but the results do not answer the question because they are only "related to" it. Sometimes a search query is poorly constructed, misspelled, or otherwise inadequate. When a Google search turns up nothing, students (and others) often assume that there is nothing to find. If they don't get an instant answer, they assume there is no answer at all.

Experienced researchers learn about a new topic by starting the search for information with a wide range of sources and then narrowing to more specific and targeted sources as they gain information. If they don't find what they are looking for in one source, they try another source. They understand that the search for information takes time and patience. It takes mental flexibility to consider who might cover the topic under consideration and to seek out sources of information from those individuals or institutions. It takes some thought to consider search terms, synonyms, alternative spellings, and other means of obtaining results. It takes time to evaluate information sources for accuracy, reliability, and applicability. It is a winding path through the forest of information possibilities, a treasure hunt that will answer a question or solve a problem. An experienced researcher knows and embraces the process, including the time it takes and the number of sources one might need to explore. For the beginner in information literacy, it is necessary to unlearn the expectation of an instant answer while learning patience and perseverance in research.

Information literacy instruction should help beginning students understand the components of the search process. Instruction should guide students through the forest of information, showing them examples of alternative sources along the way. It should also provide students with practice in independent discovery of information from a variety of sources. Instruction should help students become researchers by making the search process habitual, if not automatic. To develop this habit, it is necessary to overcome the need for speed and instead emphasize quality. Success in this rather daunting task will ultimately contribute to students' overall success in their classes, in their workplaces, and in their daily lives.

Thus far in the information age, the quantity of information available has grown astronomically. The abundance of information is both a blessing and a curse. The answer to any question is probably out there, but finding it can be next to impossible. The quality of the information available varies widely as well, placing the accurate and reliable side by side with the biased and the just-plain-wrong. The lack of governance over these many information sources places the onus on the user to evaluate the content. Users unskilled in the evaluation of information run the risk of selecting misleading, outdated, or incorrect information. Selection and use of bad information had unintended consequences before the information age. That result is unlikely to change in today's information glutted world. Students should be taught to formulate a strategy for finding information that will help them retrieve accurate and reliable sources.

In order to find information, critical thinking is, well, critical. Students need to understand that Google is not the only tool available, nor is it always the best tool to use. Students can be introduced to new or different sources of information in the appropriate situation (i.e., when the information is relevant to them). When they learn about new sources at the right time, students can readily see how alternative sources can be useful. Unfortunately many instructors assume that students either know about the range of resources available to them or can find what they need using an Internet search engine. As we have seen in library instruction, neither of these assumptions is true.

Often students don't know where to begin their search for information. They should be reminded that the first step in research is to gather background information. A Google search might be a place to gather general information, but it will also return many other types of information, not all of which will be at an introductory level. It is good to remind students about the sources of information that will provide an overview of a topic. For example, a researcher can gather some general information about a topic from an encyclopedia article. It is not the only place to look, but it is a place to begin.

It is important to emphasize to students that gathering background information on a general topic is not the same thing as finding information to answer a specific research question. The search for background information allows novices to understand the topic, to learn about its history, to discover the smaller topics that fall under its umbrella. Eventually the background information can help create a research question that can be studied in depth. Students in grade school often start projects by using encyclopedias. As they progress through the school system, they often learn about other resources. At the high school level, students are often told that encyclopedias are no longer acceptable sources. It is easy to see why students are confused about where to start their research. Information literacy instruction can help clear up the mystery by highlighting the differences between background information and other kinds of information.

Selection of terms to search is another difficult task for novice researchers. It is hard to know what words are important if relatively little is known about the subject under consideration. Students often have difficulty identifying keywords in a sentence. They also have difficulty finding synonyms for subjects that are new to them. Yet many students have never considered using a thesaurus or subject heading list, largely because they have not been guided to do so by an experienced researcher. This is another area where guided practice can instill a habit of mind that transfers from task to task in courses on different subjects, in workplace projects, and in problem solving in life.

Remember the serendipity of finding a fabulous book while you were in the stacks looking for something else? Or coming across a citation to the perfect journal article while skimming the citations in a bibliography? Or finding out about a new publication that promised to offer just the information you were looking for? This kind of searching and finding does not happen when the items on the first page of a Google search are the only information considered. Sometimes just casting around for information, trying different combinations of words and ideas, can produce remarkable results. This kind of experimentation with searching can benefit students. Students should be aware of the power of serendipity when exploring a topic or idea. Again, guidance and practice can establish the habit of creative thought and experimentation that can be transferred to other situations.

Students often overlook resources available to them because they have never learned about those resources. The bibliography in a book or journal article is often a mystery to students. They may know that the bibliography is there to protect the author against claims of plagiarism, but they typically have no understanding of what else the bibliography can do for them. As part of the process of exploration, students should learn about the chain of information and research that exists when bibliographies are linked backward from the present. This method of reaching back in time to the beginnings of an idea does not occur to most students independently. The idea that the seminal writings about a topic are cited most often in the bibliographies of the literature that comes after them should be explained to students. Finally, students often overlook the fact that the items in the bibliography of a book or article are additional sources of information on the same topic that could be used to further the inquiry. Students do not have to discover these sources on their own. The author of the book or article in hand has already identified more sources about the topic in the bibliography. Students can take advantage of the work that other authors have done by reviewing the bibliographies of the works they have in hand.

Associations and organizations often have experts who work there. A foundation for research on arthritis, for example, will often have medical experts who are associated with the organization. The American Civil Liberties Union has lawyers who are associated with the group. Valuable information about a topic can be accessed by asking for it from the experts who support an association or organization. Information from associations and organizations may need to be selected judiciously after evaluation for accuracy, reliability, and bias, depending on the institution's subject and approach to that subject. An association that supports the Second Amendment right to bear arms, for example, may only provide information about the side of the issue it supports. The student must find other information created by a group that is against the right to bear arms in order to get the full picture concerning the topic. It is also important for students to understand that the web domain name .org does not confer any trustworthiness on the group owning the website. Each website must be evaluated individually, regardless of its domain.

College students are often in the very same geographic place as noted experts in many fields—their college or university campus. Yet they do not take advantage of this proximity. Although professors and researchers are busy people, they find time to provide their expertise when called upon to do so. Students should be introduced to the experts on their home campuses and encouraged to make use of those experts when it is appropriate. Faculty members are usually willing to answer a question or two by e-mail or telephone. They may be willing to spend a short time in a face-to-face interview with a student. As experts in their fields, faculty members have almost certainly written something about their subjects. Students can use this knowledge to identify sources of information on a topic of interest. Finally, faculty are often good sources of information about others doing research in the same field. Faculty members are a remarkable resource that students could use to further their research.

NOTE

1. Association of College and Research Libraries, *Framework for Information Literacy for Higher Education* (Chicago: American Library Association, 2015), www.ala.org/acrl/standards/ilframework.

Keywords

In this exercise students will practice selecting keywords from sentences.

LEARNING OUTCOMES

- Students will learn what a keyword is.
- Students will learn to identify keywords in sentences.

The instructor should provide a definition of *keyword*. The instructor should also provide a worksheet containing five to eight sentences of varied complexity. The instructor might ask students to find a specific number of keywords in each sentence. This exercise can be done as a class or individually. If done as a class, the instructor should ask students to suggest keywords and write them on a flip chart, whiteboard, or the like. The instructor should then ask students to agree or disagree with the suggested keywords.

INSTRUCTIONS

Circle the keywords in the sentences on the worksheet provided by your instructor. Conduct a Google search using the keywords from one or two of the sentences on the worksheet. Discuss the success of the searches.

Sample Sentences

The quick brown fox jumped over the lazy dog.

Arguing every now and then is a part of a healthy marriage.

Traditional attitudes toward self-published books are changing.

By introducing "information literacy" in the workplace, employers are giving employees the opportunity to rethink and redefine the "information overload" problem itself.

George floated in the suds with the jets puckering bubbles toward his lower sacro-
iliac and sciatic nerve.

Fast-paced developments in information technology make this an interesting time
for coastal and marine database systems.

Global warming is causing migrating birds to change their habits.

Children who live in poverty are more likely to have asthma than are children who
live above the poverty line.

EXERCISE 40

Background Information

In this exercise students will learn that research begins with gathering background information about a topic.

LEARNING OUTCOMES

- Students will learn about general sources for background information.
- Students will learn about the content of general and subject-specific encyclopedias.
- Students will learn the difference between general and subject-specific encyclopedias.

Most students have used an encyclopedia at some point in their lives. Many students are astonished to learn that both general and subject-specific encyclopedias are available. The instructor should offer suggestions, including *Wikipedia*, if necessary. This exercise works best for students working individually or in pairs.

INSTRUCTIONS

Use a general encyclopedia to find an article on a topic of your choice. Read the article and summarize the content.

Identify the category into which the selected topic falls (e.g., acne—dermatology, cancer—medicine, poverty—economics, etc.).

Find a subject-specific encyclopedia for the category just identified. Look up the same topic in the subject-specific encyclopedia. Read and summarize the article.

Compare the two sources and identify and explain the differences between the two.

Why do we have both general and subject-specific encyclopedias?

EXERCISE 41

Keyword Searching in the Library Catalog

In this exercise students will learn how to find books on a topic in an online catalog or on the shelf.

LEARNING OUTCOMES

- Students will learn that books about the same topic are often shelved next to each other in the library.
- Students will learn that Amazon and other booksellers also categorize by subject.

The library's physical collection is organized by subject. Books about the same subject are classified so that they all live close together on the library shelves. This arrangement makes it easy to find materials about a specific topic. Some library online catalogs show the covers of books as they would appear on the shelf. If your catalog doesn't have this function, send students directly to the stacks.

INSTRUCTIONS

Do a search for a book in the library catalog.

What is the title of the book?

Use the function that shows the book covers and call numbers, or find the book on the library shelf. Copy the titles of the books on either side of the book searched.

What are those titles?

Are they about the same or similar topics?

Now go to Amazon.com and search for a book.

What is the title of the book?

Look at the list of similar books generated by Amazon ("Customers who bought this item also bought . . . ").

What are two of the suggested titles?

Are they about the same or similar topics?

EXERCISE 42

Defining Your Terms

Students can save themselves time and effort by thinking about the meaning of the keywords they use when searching and by understanding that a word can have different meanings in different disciplines.

LEARNING OUTCOMES

- Students will learn that different disciplines use words differently.
- Students will learn to search for keywords in the relevant discipline.

Students can use online dictionaries to complete this exercise.

INSTRUCTIONS

Using a general dictionary, look up the word "depression."

How many different meanings are listed?

In how many different disciplines is the word "depression" used?

What is the definition for "depression" in meteorology?

What is the definition for "depression" in geology?

What is the definition for "depression" in the field of psychology?

Find a dictionary of psychology (search "dictionary and psychology," for example). Read the definition in this subject-specific dictionary.

Does this definition agree with the one in the general dictionary?

Does the subject-specific dictionary give more information for this use of the word than the general dictionary?

Do a Google search for the term "depression."

How many hits did you get?

Do a Google search for the terms "depression and meteorology."

How many hits did you get?

Did limiting your search to a specific discipline help you find what you were looking for?

Using Boolean Searching

Many students do not know how to use Boolean searching. A short lesson about the mathematician Boole and the concepts of narrowing and broadening a search will engage students and give them a better understanding of the arithmetic properties involved in searching.

LEARNING OUTCOMES

- Students will learn about Boole.
- Students will learn three terms in Boolean searching—AND, OR, NOT.
- Students will learn how each term is used.
- Students will learn what effect each term has on a search.

George Boole was a Scottish mathematician who lived in the early to middle 1800s. His field was algebra. In his work he replaced the symbol for multiplication with the word AND and the symbol for addition with the word OR to create Boolean logic. Replacing the symbol with the word helped create the rules about how algebra works. Fast forward to the twentieth century and you will find that Boolean logic was used as the backbone for the creation of digital circuit design. Today Boolean logic is also used to tell a search engine like Google exactly what kind of information to look for, without the need for the questioner to have any understanding of algebra or mathematics at all!

The instructor should lead the class through this exercise. The exercise can also be done using physical characteristics of students—hair color, eye color, long- or short-sleeved shirt, skirt or pants, and so on.

INSTRUCTIONS

Step 1. Cut pieces of construction paper into a variety of large shapes—squares, triangles, and circles, for example. Use three different colors of paper. Write one of three general topics on each shape. (For example, you might have a green square with the topic "global warming" on it, a blue triangle with the topic "United States" on it, and a yellow circle with the topic "carbon" on it.) Give each student one shape of each color.

Step 2. Ask all those students with a green shape to stand. Count and record the number of students standing. Then ask all those with a green triangle to remain standing—everyone else sits down. Count and record the number of students standing. On a whiteboard or flip chart, write "green AND triangle." Ask students why the second number is smaller than the first number. Point out that using the term AND makes the search more specific and, therefore, the result smaller.

Step. 3. Ask students to stand if they have a circle. Count and record the number. Ask students who have a circle or a square to stand. Count and record the number. On a whiteboard or flip chart write "circle OR square." Ask the students to explain why the second number is now bigger. Point out that using the word OR makes the search broader so the result is bigger.

Step 4. Ask students to stand if they have a triangle. Count and record this number. Ask students in this group to sit if their triangle is blue. Count and record the result. Write on the whiteboard or flip chart "triangle NOT blue." Ask students to explain what the term NOT did to the search.

Step 5. Ask students to look for the topic words on the construction paper shapes. Ask students with a shape that says "global warming" to stand. Ask students with the terms "global warming" and "United States" to remain standing while everyone else sits down. Ask students to explain what they just accomplished (narrowed the search) and what that search would look like if they wrote it down ("global warming AND United States").

Step 6. Ask everyone with the topic "global warming" to stand again. Then ask anyone with the term "politics" to also stand. Ask students to explain what they just accomplished (broadened the search) and what that search would look like if they wrote it down ("global warming OR politics").

Step 7. Ask everyone with the topic "politics" to stand. Then ask everyone standing to sit if they also have the topic "United States." Ask students to explain what they just accomplished (eliminated an unwanted segment of information—narrowing the search) and what that search would look like if they wrote it down ("politics NOT United States").

Advanced Boolean Searching—Nested Searches

Step 1. Ask students who have the term "United States" to stand. Ask students who have "United States" and "global warming" to remain standing. Ask students who have "United States" and "global warming" and "politics" to sit. Ask students to discuss what this search would look like ("United States AND global warming NOT politics").

Step 2. Remind students of the order of mathematical calculations—numbers inside parentheses get done first.

Step 3. Put parentheses around "United States AND global warming." Ask students to explain what this search would yield (information about both the United States and global warming). Once those results are gathered, what does "NOT politics" do to the search? (It subtracts information that discusses the political aspects of global warming and the United States.)

Step 4. Ask students to put the parentheses around "global warming NOT politics." Then ask them how this search is different from the previous search.

Beyond Keywords

Students usually start their research using keywords. Without further instruction this is probably as far as they will go. To show them other ways of manipulating information to search, explain the subject search concept and the author/title search concept.

LEARNING OUTCOMES

- Students will learn that there are multiple ways to access information by searching different fields in online records.
- Students will learn how to conduct a subject search and a title search.

The instructor should lead the class through this exercise or allow students to work independently.

INSTRUCTIONS: PART 1

Do a keyword search in the library catalog using the keyword "automobile." Note the number of results.

How many results did you get?

Look at the first page of results to get a general sense of the kinds of information this search generated.

Are the items retrieved specifically about automobiles?

List all the synonyms you can think of for the keyword "automobile" (e.g., car, horseless carriage, transport vehicle, sedan, compact, roadster, etc.).

1.

2.

3.

Do keyword searches for words on the list.

How many searches did you do?

In the keyword search for "automobile," the results included only items with the word "automobile" somewhere in the record. Then you had to search for the word "sedan." Then you had to search for "roadster." The computer will only give you results that include the keyword you use. In a keyword search, each word has to be searched individually to find all the relevant information about all the different words for "automobile."

Choose one of the terms on the list of words to represent them all.

The *subject* term for all the automobile terms on the list is: _____

Every computer record in the library catalog has a subject field. The subject term like the one you just chose would be put in a special place in the electronic record for each item the library owns whose subject is "automobile," "car," "roadster," "horseless carriage," or any other synonym you came up with.

Now, try the subject search in the library's catalog or in a journal database. (This usually involves using a drop-down menu on which you can select the type of search you want to do.) Do a subject search using your subject term for "automobile." Note the number of hits.

How many hits did you get?

Note that all the hits deal with automobiles, even if the word does not appear in the record. Using the subject search function is more efficient than using the keyword search because you only have to search one term rather than keyword searching many terms.

INSTRUCTIONS: PART 2

How do you know what word is used to stand for the term you are looking for and its synonyms? Look for the subject list in the library catalog or the database you are searching and click on it to get to the index. Search for your topic ("automobile").

Does the database use the term you looked for?

If yes, what are the terms above and below your term? Are they related to your term?

If no, what term does the database use instead of the term you used?

Go back to the database search screen. Do a subject search using the subject term from the subject list. Compare the results you get from this search with the results from the keyword search.

Did one search find more information than the other?

Which type of search gave more results that are specific to the topic?

INSTRUCTIONS: PART 3

Every item in the library online catalog has a title. There is a field in every computer record for title. A title often indicates what a publication is about. *Introduction to Psychology* is probably about psychology. *Statistical Tips and Tricks* is probably about statistics. Identifying a keyword of interest and searching for that keyword in the title may help you find material on the topic.

Use the keyword "automobile" in the title search function. (By doing a title search, you are asking the computer to look in that specific field only.)

How many titles had the word "automobile"?

This kind of searching is helpful if you don't know the exact title of a book, but you know one or more of the words in the title. Of course, if you know the exact title of the book you are looking for, using the title search function is much more efficient than using a keyword or subject search.

Compare and contrast the results for each of the subject and title searches.

You have considered keyword, subject, and title searches.

What other kinds of searches would be helpful?

You can use combinations of keywords, authors, titles, and so on. Try combining your keyword with a specific person (painting/Monet).

How many results did you get?

EXERCISE 45

Using a Thesaurus to Generate Search Terms

Students know that words often have synonyms. The word they use for something may not be the only term for the same concept. How does one find out what other words mean the same thing? To identify synonyms, students will learn to use a thesaurus. They will generate a list of synonyms for a topic.

LEARNING OUTCOMES

- Students will learn how to use a thesaurus.
- Students will learn to search for multiple keywords in a database.

The instructor may provide a hard copy or online thesaurus.

INSTRUCTIONS

Select a one-word topic.

What is your topic?

Using a thesaurus, look up your topic. Generate a list of synonyms for your topic.

What are synonyms for your topic?

Using a journal database, perform a keyword search for your original topic.

How many articles did you find?

Now do a keyword search using one of your synonyms.

How many articles did you find?

Compare the two lists of articles.

Are the articles on the first list the same as the articles on the second list?

In the search screen of the database, use both the original topic and the synonym you selected. Type the two words in the same search box separated with the word OR (e.g., red OR blue), or type the first word in the first search box and type the second word in the second box and connect the two boxes with the word OR.

Complete the search. Look at the articles on the list and compare them to the articles you found in your previous two searches.

Are the articles from the first two searches all included in the third list?

Who Has Information?

Knowing who might produce needed information can make it easier to find that information. Brainstorming about who collects different kinds of information is a useful exercise and can help students think about alternate sources of information. (See also exercise 18 in chapter 3, "Research as Inquiry.")

LEARNING OUTCOMES

- Students will learn to brainstorm about who produces information.
- Students will learn to consider who produces certain types of information.

The instructor should provide a list of questions and ask students to determine who would have the information.

INSTRUCTIONS

Think of two different people, groups, or organizations who could produce an answer to the following questions:

How many square miles are in Rhode Island? (examples of sources: state government, *Wikipedia*, Google maps)

    1.

    2.

What are the rules for polling places (places where people vote) in Rhode Island? (examples of sources: state government, federal government, Board of Canvassers, League of Women Voters)

    1.

    2.

How many people died from gunshot wounds in the United States in 2010? (examples of sources: National Rifle Association, federal government, local government, hunting groups, police)

    1.

    2.

How long will it be before the polar ice caps melt?

     1.
     2.

What crimes were committed at elementary schools in Michigan in 2015?

     1.
     2.

How many different kinds of cancer are there?

     1.
     2.

Search Google for sources of information about the preceding topics and find the answers. (For example, Google "square miles in RI" and get the result. Then Google "polling places" and find the rules governing polling places, and so on.) Note the source of the information, including the URL. Also note how many tries it took to find a website with the correct or wanted information.

Database Smorgasbord

LEARNING OUTCOMES

- Students will learn that different databases cover different subjects and different sources.
- Students will learn to consider and select appropriate databases for their research subject.

Students often stick with using the tools they already know rather than experimenting with new sources of information. The content of proprietary databases is often unknown and unexplored simply because students do not know these databases exist. Because libraries pay lots of money to subscribe to databases, it is in our best interest to, at the very least, teach students about their existence.

INSTRUCTIONS

Start at the library home page. Find the link on the library home page that will take you to the list of databases available.

How are the databases listed (e.g., alphabetically, by subject, by discipline, etc.)?

Read the description for a general database.

What topics are covered?

Read the description for a subject-specific database.

What topics are covered?

If you were looking for general information to get started on a topic, which database might be more useful to you?

If you wanted information specific to a medical topic, which database might be more useful to you?

Click on the link for a general database. Click on the link that shows the titles of the publications included in the database.

What kinds of publications (e.g., newspapers, magazines, journals, book chapters, etc.) are included?

Click on the link for a subject-specific database. Click on the link that shows the titles of the publications included in the database.

What kinds of publications are included?

Do a search for a topic in a general database.

How many results did you get?

How many of the results on the first page are relevant to what you were looking for?

Do the same search in an appropriate subject-specific database.

How many results did you get?

How many of the results on the first page are relevant to what you were looking for?

When would you use a general database?

When would you use a subject-specific database?

Experts and Interviews

LEARNING OUTCOMES

- Students will learn to consider individuals who are sources of information and where to find them.
- Students will learn how to conduct an in-person interview with an expert.
- Students will learn about experts available to them in the academic setting.

The instructor should be ready to help students match their topics with appropriate academic disciplines.

INSTRUCTIONS

Select a research topic.

What academic department(s) in your college or university would cover your topic or some aspect of your topic?

Go to the web page for that department and look at the biographical information about the faculty in that department.

Are there any faculty listed who have an interest in or teach a class on your topic?

Imagine you have made an appointment to interview one of the faculty members you just identified about your topic. Make a list of questions you would ask at that interview.

1.
2.
3.

Now consider how you would write a citation for your interview with your selected faculty member. After consulting the appropriate style guide for format, write your citation for an in-person interview with Professor X.

EXERCISE 49

Associations and Organizations

LEARNING OUTCOMES

- Students will learn how to identify associations and organizations.
- Students will learn that associations and organizations may be sources for information.

Associations and organizations are often sources of information about topics of special interest. For example, Mothers Against Drunk Driving (MADD) will have information about drunk driving and the effects of drunk driving. The association collects statistics and other information concerning drunk driving. Some groups have experts in the association or affiliated with the association who provide the information they share. Part of MADD's mission is to educate people about drunk driving, so the organization will have information to share on that topic. (Given the name of the group, it is clear that the group has a bias against drunk driving, so that outlook will be a factor when evaluating the information the group provides.)

INSTRUCTIONS

Select a topic. Do an Internet search for organizations that have something to do with your topic. Select two organizations relevant to your research topic. Look for a .org domain designation.

What are the URLs for those organizations?

1.
2.

Answer the following questions for each organization:

Who belongs to the organization?

Who runs the group? How is it organized? How is it supported?

Does the organization list credentialed experts as members?

Does another group or agency sponsor the website?

What information does the organization offer?

Does the information provided appear to be biased in any way?

If the organization supports one side of a controversial argument, does it provide any information explaining what the other side of the argument is?

Can you verify any of the information offered? (Did you find the same information in another source?)

Can you contact someone at the organization directly?

Would information from this organization be useful to your research?

EXERCISE 50

Strategizing

LEARNING OUTCOMES

- Students will learn to plan a strategy for finding information.
- Students will learn to test that strategy and evaluate the results.
- Students will learn to modify their strategy based on the first test.

The instructor should pose a research question to students and ask them to create a strategic plan for finding information about that topic.

INSTRUCTIONS

You will be doing research on a question provided by your instructor. Before beginning your research, create a strategic plan for finding information on this topic.

Can you define the terms in the topic? If not, what dictionary will you use to define the terms you don't know?

Is there only one definition for the topic, or do different disciplines use the same term to mean different things?

What are the keywords you will use to search for this topic? How will you specify the definition you want to use in your search?

What are synonyms you will use to search for this topic? Where will you find synonyms?

Where would background information on this topic be published?

What are three information sources you could use to get started on this topic?

1.
2.
3.

Search the sources you listed and summarize what you learned about the topic.

Did any of the sources provide you with new leads about who might provide research on this topic and where it is located? Name one or two people or organizations.

What other information sources will provide more specific information? Are there databases or websites that specialize in information on this topic? Name one or two new sources of information.

Are there any authors whose names appear repeatedly in your search on this topic?

Did you discover new keywords that will help with your search?

Based on what you now know, do you need to revise your search strategy to find the information you need?

chapter 7

Information Has Value

"**I**NFORMATION POSSESSES SEVERAL DIMENSIONS OF VALUE, INCLUDING AS A commodity, as a means of education, as a means to influence, and as a means of negotiating and understanding the world. Legal and socioeconomic interests influence information production and dissemination."[1] Sometimes it seems like we are adrift in an ocean of free information. We turn on the computer or the television and we are instantly connected to countless sources of information. It is easy to forget that information is gathered, written, and published by people who make their living that way. Much of the information we see that appears to be free has costs that are not directly visible to the viewer. For example, in one current business model for information on the Internet, advertisers pay for space on websites where they can deliver their advertising message. This practice allows the website owners to support the cost of having a website without asking their followers to pay for it. It also allows advertisers to reach the audience of that website. This means that Internet users who go to the website do not have to pay for it directly. This does not mean the website is free! Information is often a commodity, and someone pays to make it available.

Another way to think about information and its value is to consider how many students attend college to learn the information in a particular field and to take advantage of the knowledge of the faculty experts in that field. Education is a means of extracting value from information. It makes information meaningful and applicable and provides practice to students in the selection and use of information. Once students have received their education on a particular topic, they are considered prepared to enter the workforce and apply their education to a job. Paying for the requisite information needed to begin a career is another way that information has value.

Many writers earn their living by collecting information and writing about what they find. Reporters, biographers, college professors, novelists, historians, columnists, bloggers, and others support themselves with this kind of work. Publishers also earn their living by publishing the information the writers create. People who lay out a newspaper or magazine issue, illustrators, copy editors, and others also earn their livelihood by this system. The sale of the information supports both the process and the people who make it happen. The information they provide has value for its consumers.

Information can be used as a means to influence others. Providing and withholding information give power to the person who controls the information. A small group may control information vital to the well-being of others. By sharing or withholding information, the group's members gain power and status and are often placed in positions as rulers. By acting as gatekeepers of information, the rulers influence what others know and therefore influence what others can do. In the precolonial world of Mexico, those people who knew something about astronomy could predict astronomical events. By controlling the information about astronomical events and their causes, these specialists were able to gain power over those who were less informed. In the world today, governments can limit what their people can see on the Internet. Newspaper publishers can choose which stories to report and which to ignore. Publishers of scholarly journals can require that authors sign over their copyright and then require those same authors to pay to use their own information. Control over information can be used for good or evil, for self-gain or the benefit of humanity. In this sense information has value.

Information helps us understand our world, our place in the world and the worlds beyond the world we know. Those with little information have little knowledge of the world. In a recent posting on the Facebook site "Humans of New York," one man summed up how information and education changed his worldview:

> My grandfather was a laborer, but he paid to send my father to a tutor so that he could learn to read. He told my father that, if nothing else, he should begin by learning how to read and write his name. When I was born, my father taught me how to read. I started with local newspapers. I learned that our village was part of a country. Then I moved on to books. And I learned that there was an entire world around this mountain. I learned about human rights. Now I'm studying political science at the local university. I want to be a teacher. (www.facebook.com/humansofnewyork)

This man's story is a prime example of the value of information. Where education is not available, access to and use of information is almost irrelevant.

In countries where information is blocked, even the well-educated individual cannot make use of it. If the government of a country does not allow access to different political points of view, the people of that country will not know that there are other ways of living and organizing society. There are many marginalized and underrepresented voices in the world. Part of the cause for this marginalization is a lack of information.

Many students in privileged situations can't imagine life without the information that allows them their place in the world. The fact that some people simply don't have the information they need because they don't have the means to access it is a foreign concept to the privileged. Children who have grown up with unfettered access to information often don't realize that the same is not true everywhere. There is an assumption that because everything on the Internet is available to them, everyone has access to it. The truth is that access to information is uneven. According to a Pew Research Center study in 2013, "90 percent of college graduates had high-speed Internet access, compared to less than 34 percent of those who had not finished high school. . . . Hispanic and African American students are significantly less likely to have a broadband connection at home than Caucasian or Asian American students."[2]

As these statistics show, millions of people in the United States do not have access to the Internet at home. The lack of access deprives those people of the value of the information others take for granted. Many people who lack higher education also lack high-speed Internet access. The people who earn the lowest wages often cannot afford to pay the high price for access to the information they might use to improve their lives. Students of color are less likely to be able to compete with white students because they don't have the same access to information. Unequal Internet access to information is further exacerbated by the fact that much information is now produced only in electronic format. This limitation makes it even more difficult for the have-nots because the paper copies of some kinds of information can no longer substitute for the electronic versions. Electronic information is not easily available to those who cannot afford to pay for access. This situation creates a two-tiered system whose ethical implications are disturbing.

On an even broader scale, the same Pew study reports that "On a global level, only about one-third of the world's population has access to the Internet."[3] As more and more information becomes digital-only, the gap between those with access and those without access grows ever wider. This disparity in turn often widens the gap between the rich and the poor, the healthy and the sick, the haves and the have-nots. The value of information clearly has a moral or ethical side to be considered.

COPYRIGHT VERSUS FAIR USE

For people who earn their living by producing and disseminating information, it is important that their work be legally protected. The force of law allows authors to "own" their work, even if their work consists only of ideas rather than tangible materials. The term *copyright* means that the author has the right to own and sell the "copy" (the information) she has produced. This restriction means that no one else can take or claim that work. The enforcement of the protection of intellectual property varies from country to country, making the rights of authors somewhat unstable, but in most places the rights of the creators of information are well understood and respected.

Copyright was established to protect the owners of intellectual property—ideas, music, lyrics, and so on. Without legal protection anyone could claim to have written the Harry Potter books or the words to the "Star-Spangled Banner" or the music for the song "My Sweet Lord." The authors of these works earn their living from the sales of these intellectual properties. If someone else claimed to be the author and sold the intellectual property (the story, the music, the lyrics), that person would be stealing the profits from the rightful owner and is subject to penalty by law. In the United States, under most conditions, the rights of the copyright holder are protected, and no one may use copyrighted material without express permission from the owner. The law concerning copyright varies from country to country, however. It is very difficult to stop copyright infringement across international boundaries.

In certain circumstances, the rights of the copyright holder are set aside for the benefit of the many. U.S. copyright law states that a copy or copies of an author's work may be used, without charge, in some instances. This practice is known as "fair use." In education, for example, in order to teach a subject, it is sometimes necessary to use someone else's work to inform, explain, or exemplify a topic for a group of students. If each student had to pay to view each piece of information used in a class, education would be exponentially more expensive and out of reach for many. In research, if previous research was only available by purchase, the pace of research would be glacial, and only those who could afford to pay for the information would be able to move the research process forward. For this reason, copyright law allows a few exceptions to the protections conferred on the owners of the copyright.

U.S. copyright also has a time limit attached to it, allowing the author to receive the financial benefit of the copyright protection during a period long enough to cover the life of the author and the author's descendants, but not forever. Once the time limit has passed, the information passes into the public domain, and anyone can use it without charge.

Sometimes, in order to get information published, the author has to sign away his copyright to the publisher. When this happens, ownership of the information transfers to the publisher. The publisher owns the rights and can do what it wants with the information. This transfer of copyright is one way authors can make sure their information gets produced so that people will be able to see and make use of it. However, it also gives publishers the ability to limit access to the information. If a publisher owns the copyright to all the research done in biotechnology, for example, that publisher can then ask those who want to work in the field of biotechnology to pay to see the previous research. This practice significantly disadvantages those who cannot afford to pay and requires authors to pay to use their own work in some cases.

OPEN ACCESS

A new movement in research and education is trying to change the way copyrighted information is published. This movement is known as the open access movement. Traditional publishers provide a platform where information is made available to those who want to buy it at the price the publisher sets. Open access publications are funded differently, often asking the author or the organization sponsoring the research to pay the costs of publishing the information, but allowing the author to keep the copyright. The costs for publishing are often subsidized. Publications are often "not for profit" enterprises. Low overhead and the distributed costs of publication make the process more affordable. This means that the information can be offered to the public without the cost barrier of traditional publication. It allows the author to maintain her rights to the information, and it allows information to be disseminated more quickly. It even allows taxpayers to reap the benefit of the tax dollars that go to government research by allowing everyone to see what those tax dollars have produced.

THE PUBLIC DOMAIN

Once the information enters the public domain—that is, once the copyright has run out—anyone may use it freely and without specific permission. Information that enters the public domain is old information. Older information is often only available in the format in which it was originally produced. Many older writings, for example, have only been available in paper format. This means that in order to use the material, one must go to the place where the information is housed. Much information that is no longer copyright protected has been housed in library collections throughout the world. Although this practice preserves older materials, access to those materials is limited or, in some cases, impossible. Not everyone can afford to travel to the place where the information resides. Sometimes the information resides where access is restricted and even if one could afford to go, the information would not be available. Sadly, much information has been lost because no library chose to preserve it. Finally, some information has been lost because the only copy was destroyed.

Recently several groups have set out to make access to materials in the public domain possible through the Internet. Project Gutenberg, begun in the 1990s, set out to make the contents of out-of-copyright books available to anyone with Internet access. Volunteers typed the contents of books, word for word, into computer files that were then made available at the Project Gutenberg website. When scanning became both possible and common, the content of books was scanned, rather than typed. The volunteers now verify the quality of the scans and correct any problems before the book is released. With the advent of OCR (optical character recognition) technology whereby the computer can actually recognize words, many of the books are now searchable as well as readable. The ability to search for a specific word or phrase in a large number of writings could be invaluable to future researchers.

Google Books is another project that set out to scan and make available information about all books and, under certain conditions, to make the content of those books available online. It is a project to create a catalog of the world's books and to make their locations, availability, and accessibility easy.

> The Library Project's aim is simple: make it easier for people to find relevant books—specifically, books they wouldn't find any other way such as those that are out of print—while carefully respecting authors' and publishers' copyrights. Our ultimate goal is to work with publishers and libraries to create a comprehensive, searchable, virtual card catalog of all books in all languages that helps users discover new books and publishers discover new readers. (www.google.com/googlebooks/library/)

Many books are no longer in print, which can make it difficult to access the information in them. It can be difficult to locate a copy of an out-of-print book and harder still to get to the place where it resides. Thus, the information is effectively locked away from the vast majority of possible users. Google Books Library Project strives to collect and disseminate information about where to find books and, where allowed by law, to make the content of books available on the Internet. Although not everyone on the planet has access to the Internet, providing access to information on the Internet exponentially increases the number of people who can get to it.

The HathiTrust Digital Library, founded in 2008, focuses on the preservation and sharing of digitized information. This group of cooperating institutions works with other groups like Google Books to provide a safe digital location for long-term preservation of the material they own. Such protection is especially important for "born digital" materials, as they have no paper counterpart. This effort will ensure that the shared digital information will not disappear or become inaccessible as technology changes. Protection and preservation of "born digital" materials is a new and growing problem. The HathiTrust Digital Library is an early solution to the preservation of a small part of those materials, but the need for preservation on an exponentially larger scale will keep information specialists busy for a long time.

PLAGIARISM

Plagiarism is the act of claiming intellectual property that belongs to someone else. By failing to cite the author of an idea, a student or researcher plagiarizes, giving the impression that the idea was his own. This action detracts from the benefit due the original author for doing the work. It gives credit where it doesn't belong. So plagiarizing hurts the original author and inappropriately benefits the person who claims the idea as his own (or fails to say the idea is not his own). In some cases the harm done to the legitimate author is financial. If the information is a commodity being sold—copies of a book, for example—the profits should go to the person who originally wrote the words. If someone else claims the book as his own and gets money for selling that book, the effect is essentially the same as stealing the money from the author. When the plagiarism has an economic impact on the author, the U.S. legal system can be called into play. If money is not a factor, the loss to the author who has been plagiarized may be measured in terms of prestige and recognition. In all cases, even when there is little or no money involved, the issue is moral. It is just wrong to claim someone else's ideas as one's own.

PLAGIARISM AND CITATION

When making use of someone else's work, especially in the academic and research worlds, a writer, researcher, or student must give credit to that author by citing where the information came from, regardless of how old the information might be. Such citation creates links between current research and the original idea about the topic. It is particularly useful for researchers to follow an idea back to its inception and to see what work others have done concerning the same topic. Citation is also the means of giving credit to those whose work was used to produce new work.

Enough information must be revealed in a citation to allow a reader to find the original information. The citation information required varies for different information formats. For example, a book citation contains five basic elements: author, title, place of publication, name of the publisher, and date of publication. For a film, the required pieces of information are different, because the way a film is created is different. For music, still another group of elements is required. The citation for information that comes from a website looks different than a citation for information that comes from an audio file. Many disciplines have their own rules about citation formats. For example, the American Psychological Association has a specific citation format that is different from the citation format of the Modern Language Association.

The more value a copyrighted item has, the more likely it is that using that material without permission will be punished, either through the legal system or by other means. A singing group called The Chiffons sang a song called "He's So Fine" in the 1960s. Sometime after that George Harrison produced a song called "My Sweet Lord." Although his lyrics were different, the music was exactly the same. Harrison was fined more than $1 million for using the music without permission. Michael Bolton paid a fine of $5.4 million for claiming a 1966 song by the Isley Brothers as his own work.

Vladimir Putin was accused of using parts of a chapter from a 1978 textbook in his graduate thesis. His punishment was political embarrassment. In 2003 reporter Jayson Blair was found to have plagiarized material in thirty-six of the seventy-three articles he wrote for the *New York Times.* He lost his job. More recently, Republican Vaughn Ward plagiarized from Barack Obama's well-known speech to the 2004 Democratic National Convention. Ward had to withdraw his candidacy for political office. On the other side of the aisle, Democratic Senator John Walsh was accused of using a large chunk of uncited material in his final paper as a graduate student at the Army War College. He lost his degree from that institution. It is clear that even when the plagiarism does not substantially detract from the original author's income, the ethical breach can result in substantial punishment for the plagiarist.

Students live in a cut-and-paste world. It is very easy to "borrow" ideas from here and there and to forget that those ideas actually belong to someone else. In many cases, student plagiarism results from a lack of mindfulness about ownership of information. So much information is available and access to information (for some) is so effortless, it appears that information is simply there for the taking. Many high schools offer some instruction to students about plagiarism and how to avoid it, and this instruction sometimes continues in higher education. However, the instruction is often superficial or spotty—some students get it while others do not. In some cases, plagiarism is completely accidental. It is, after all, hard to say something in a completely original way. In other cases, plagiarism is simply the result of sloppy research. And in still other cases, students don't even know that use of another person's work, without attribution, is a problem. This is why it is so important to teach students when and how to cite correctly.

With the advent of fast and large computer systems, it has become fairly easy to spot plagiarism. Software that has been built to catch instances of plagiarism looks for similarities in word patterns. The larger the similarity in the word patterns, the more likely the plagiarism. Google has been used effectively to compare groups of words to an astounding number of Internet documents, allowing instructors to document possible cases of plagiarism. Most institutions have policies and punishments in place for students who plagiarize. Better instruction about information ownership and correct citation would help students understand and avoid plagiarism.

PERSONAL INFORMATION

Personal information has value to companies and institutions. By supplying your personal information online, you give something of value to someone else. Your information can be used for sales pitches, demographic studies, advertising, market research, and scams, both by the original requestor and by anyone the original requestor cares to share with. In some cases the information you provide is simply used for demographic purposes. For example, a store might want to know how many people from Wisconsin bought its products. Store leaders might want to know how many males or females, what age groups, what ethnicities bought the company's products. This type of information collection is simple counting. It helps the company, and it doesn't hurt you. Other groups track your purchases by connecting the information you supply with purchases made. Such linking is done in the guise of helping you by providing the opportunity to get information about similar products. At the individual level, this practice seems harmless enough. However, on a grand data-mining scale, it is a bit daunting. Tracking what millions of people are doing online, what products they are buying, what websites they are visiting comes to feel like an invasion of privacy, especially when the tracking is done by government agencies. Companies that collect information for benign purposes may sell that information to other companies whose motives are not so innocent.

Third-party web tracking allows companies to monitor or track our use of the Internet—what sites we go to, how long we spend there, how we search, and how many times we go back. This monitoring is all accomplished with the help of a small piece of coding known as a cookie. The cookie is loaded onto your browser when you visit a website. With the cookie in place, the next time you go to the same site, you are recognized as having been there before. The website can then amaze you by providing whatever information you left at that site the last time you were there. This feature can be helpful if you shop at a particular website often. Information you might have to supply in order to buy something can be automatically reproduced for you, thanks to the cookie. However, some cookies also allow companies to build a profile of your visits to their and other websites. Internet social media sites allow companies to put tracking cookies on their websites. When you use your social media account, your activities there may also be tracked by means of cookies. By linking personal information from a social media site with information from other websites, third-party trackers can identify specific individuals. This ability is troubling in that it is unclear what the third party can or will do with the information.

Privacy rules, or at least the practices surrounding them, are changing, and it is up to the individual to weigh the impact of divulging information. Keeping abreast of what each company, bank, store, or software program might do with the information you provide is tedious. Explanations can be hard to find and read, and they are often written in language that is hard to understand. Privacy terms are often buried in the licensing agreements we accept in order to use computer software packages, online banking products, Amazon accounts, and so on. Nobody reads the licensing agreements every time a Java upgrade appears on the computer screen, yet our privacy depends on those agreements.

In a world where terrorism is rampant, citizens of the United States have been willing to give up some privacy in order to allow government agencies to screen for terrorist activity. In a world where time seems to be in short supply, people often opt to divulge information without reading anything about what the information will be used for. In a world where everyone seems to be collecting personal information, it becomes almost automatic to answer personal questions before making a purchase in person or online. Despite warnings about scams and hackers, in the online environment we often give away valuable information about ourselves without knowing how that information might be used. Sometimes the gathering of personal information is benign, but not always. Students need instruction in questioning data collection. They need to become aware that caution is necessary when sharing information. (It is one thing to share information with a close friend. It is something else to have that friend share your information with hundreds of other friends on social media.)

NOTES

1. Association of College and Research Libraries, *Framework for Information Literacy for Higher Education* (Chicago: American Library Association, 2015), www.ala.org/acrl/standards/ilframework.

2. John Palfrey, *Biblio Tech: Why Libraries Matter More Than Ever in the Age of Google* (New York: Basic Books, 2015), 30.

3. Ibid.

Citation Styles

In this exercise students will cite a book and a journal article using American Psychological Association (APA) style and Modern Language Association (MLA) style. Students will compare the two formats and discuss possible reasons for the differences.

LEARNING OUTCOMES

- Students will learn how to create book citations in MLA and APA style.
- Students will learn how to create journal citations in MLA and APA style.
- Students will learn the differences between the elements required for citing different kinds of publications.
- Students will learn the reasons for the existence of different citation styles.

This exercise can be done in small groups or individually. The instructor should provide a book and a journal article or have students provide their own. The instructor will provide a worksheet on which students can create their citations and will either provide a computer link to the APA and MLA citation styles, create a handout with examples, or project the examples on a screen for the entire class.

The instructor should explain to students that citations for different types of information (online journals, book chapters, movies, TV shows, interviews, etc.) include different elements. The instructor should make sure that students are aware of resources that will help them learn how to create citations for various types of materials. The following process can be repeated for as many formats as needed. (Web citations, for example, are particularly different, and students could benefit from learning how to create a citation for a website.)

INSTRUCTIONS

Citations are created so that someone using that citation can locate the same publication. Using the worksheet provided by your instructor, create citations for a book and a journal article in APA style and in MLA style.

Think about possible reasons for the differences between the two styles, taking into consideration the disciplines that use each style and the information that might be most important for researchers in those disciplines to have first. Write down your thoughts or discuss your reasons with the class.

Worksheet

Step 1. Looking at the title page and verso of the book you are working with, write down the information you think would be important for creating a citation.

Step 2. Compare the information you selected with the information given in the APA format example provided by your instructor. Write down any information you missed in step 1.

Step 3. Use the APA format example to create a correctly formatted citation for the book.

Step 4. Using the information you collected in step 1 and the MLA citation format example provided by your instructor, write your citation again in MLA format.

Step 5. Look at the journal article you are working with. Write down the information you think would be important for creating a citation.

Step 6. Compare the information you wrote in step 5 with the APA format example provided by your instructor. Write down any information you missed.

Step 7. Using the information you collected in step 5 and the MLA citation format example provided by your instructor, write your citation again in MLA format.

Step 8. Comparing the two formats, identify how the citation styles differ. (Look at placement of the elements, punctuation, use of abbreviations, etc.)

EXERCISE 52

Citation Format Comparison

LEARNING OUTCOME

- Students will learn the differences between two citation styles.

The instructor will provide pairs of citations for books, journals, and websites in MLA style and APA style.

INSTRUCTIONS

List as many differences as you can between the two citation styles. List as many reasons as you can think of that might explain why the two formats are different. Then answer the following questions:

Who might use APA style citations?

Who might use MLA style citations?

What priorities might scholars using APA style citations have compared with the priorities of scholars using MLA style citations?

Journal Cost Comparison

This exercise will help students understand the cost of access to some kinds of information. This exercise can be done individually, in small groups, or as a class.

LEARNING OUTCOMES

- Students will learn about the cost of a magazine subscription and the cost of a scholarly journal subscription.
- Students will learn about individual and corporate subscription costs for a scholarly journal.
- Students will learn why there is a pricing differential between personal subscriptions and corporate subscriptions.
- Students will learn why there is a pricing differential between magazines and scholarly journals.
- Students will understand why the subscription price might limit the ability to access the information.

The instructor will provide a chart listing the cost of an annual subscription to a popular magazine (e.g., *Time, Newsweek, Cosmopolitan, Men's Health,* etc.) and a scholarly journal (e.g., *American Psychologist, American Journal of Psychiatry, International Journal of Pharmaceutics, Peace and Conflict,* etc.). The chart will include the cost of an annual individual issue purchase (that is, what it would cost to buy each issue of the publication at a newsstand for a year), an annual membership subscription, and an annual corporate subscription to one or more scholarly journals. Students will then compare costs between popular and scholarly publications and between personal and corporate subscriptions.

	INDIVIDUAL ISSUE	MEMBER	CORPORATE
Time	$20	—	—
Newsweek	$100	—	—
Men's Health	$40	—	—
American Psychologist	$419	$12	$1,399
American Journal of Psychiatry	$294	$294	—
International Journal of Pharmaceutics	$800	—	$12,320
Peace and Conflict	$74	$133	$840

INSTRUCTIONS

Compare the subscription rates provided by your instructor and answer the following questions:

Why do subscriptions to popular magazines cost less than subscriptions to scholarly journals?

Why do corporate subscriptions cost more than individual subscriptions?

How does the cost of a subscription to a publication impact access to it for an individual?

How does the cost of a subscription to a publication impact access to it for a corporate body like a library?

Is It Free?

LEARNING OUTCOMES

- Students will learn that the Internet is not free.
- Students will learn the costs for the Internet and consider how they are paid.

The instructor will select a website for students to examine.

INSTRUCTIONS

Look at the website selected by your instructor. Discuss with your classmates the costs of the website and who pays for each of the following:

- Design
- Software
- Domain name
- Upkeep and maintenance
- Advertising
- Subscription or membership
- Internet connectivity
- Computers, tablets, phones used to access
- Servers

EXERCISE 55

Plagiarism

Students in college often treat plagiarism as a minor offense that can be brushed off lightly. This exercise will help them see that there are consequences for plagiarism.

LEARNING OUTCOMES

- Students will learn about one instance of plagiarism and its consequences.
- Students will learn about some long-term effects of plagiarism.

The instructor may want to point out the institution's rules regarding plagiarism.

INSTRUCTIONS

Find out and summarize what one of the following people did regarding plagiarism and how it affected their lives:

- Kaavya Viswanathan
- Doris Kearns Goodwin
- Mike Barnicle
- James Frey

EXERCISE 56

Personal Information and Privacy

Students often give away their personal information automatically and mechanically, without thinking about who is asking or what the person or company might do with that information.

LEARNING OUTCOMES

- Students will learn about how personal information is gathered by companies, government agencies, and the like.
- Students will learn how that information has value for the groups that collect it.

This exercise can be done in small groups or as a class.

INSTRUCTIONS

Think about information requests made by a store and by the U.S. Census Bureau and answer the following questions. Compare and contrast the two forms of collecting information.

Courtesy Card

In order to obtain a courtesy card for a grocery store or drugstore, you are usually required to fill out an application.

What information is requested?

Is that information publicly available elsewhere?

What benefit do you get from having the courtesy card?

What benefit does the company get?

What happens when a grocery store or drugstore links your purchases to your courtesy card?

For you:

For the company:

What happens when the grocery store or drugstore sells your information to another company?

Visit www.epic.org and look for the information about courtesy cards.

U.S. Census

Do a Google search to find out the purpose for the census. Do a Google search to find out who has access to the information collected.

What information does the Census Bureau collect?

What is the information used for?

Is the information used by any other agency?

Is the information sold to any other group?

"In addition to collecting population data for the purposes of accurately apportioning congressional districts, the federal government uses census data, among other reasons, to determine: the allocation of federal funding for education programs in states and communities" (www.thisnation.com/question/022.html).

Social Media and Privacy

Students often share their private information on social media without considering the consequences.

LEARNING OUTCOMES

- Students will learn about privacy considerations.
- Students will learn how social media use their information.

The instructor will provide two articles about Facebook—one positive and one negative.

INSTRUCTIONS

Step 1. Create a list of pros and cons from the two articles provided by your instructor.

Step 2. Identify what information is being collected and shared by Facebook and how that information is being used. Discuss possible consequences.

Step 3. Discuss what information can be shared by others about you. Discuss the possible consequences.

EXERCISE 58

Privacy Issues

LEARNING OUTCOMES

- Students will learn about privacy issues.
- Students will consider how privacy issues impact their lives.

This exercise should be done in small groups.

INSTRUCTIONS

Log on to the website epic.org (Electronic Privacy Information Center). At the bottom of the home page is a list of Hot Policy Issues. Investigate an issue and report back to the class.

What is EPIC?

Who is in charge of EPIC?

What is your hot topic issue?

Why is this issue a privacy concern?

What is the impact on everyday life?

Does this issue have any impact on your life?

chapter 8

Creating Exercises, Rubrics, Learning Outcomes, and Learning Assessments

T WO IMPORTANT THINGS NEED TO HAPPEN TO MAKE INFORMATION LITER-acy useful to students during and after their experience in higher education. One involves making memories that stick, and the other is transfer of learning from the classroom to real life. Instruction should be designed with these two things in mind.

The human brain is complex and largely unknown. Recent research has shown some promising insights into how memory works—new knowledge that can impact what we teach and how we teach it. The brain appears to be hardwired to generalize what it sees in order to quickly relate similar things and situations. That means that the brain will try to relate a new situation or new information to something it already knows. The brain asks, how is this thing like other things I have seen before? If there are memories that seem to apply to the new situation, the brain considers that information first. The more similar the new thing is to the previous thing, the easier it is to make the connection. If there is nothing exactly the same, the brain will look for memories that closely resemble the new information. If there is no closely related memory to recall, the brain sometimes makes a leap from something that might seem unrelated by looking at its components or overarching concepts and creating an analogy.

Basic information is stored across lots of different parts of the brain. Having information stored in more than one part of the brain helps make the information more easily retrievable. Memory has at least two functional parts—working memory and long-term memory. Working memory is useful for holding new information. It works in the short term. It requires the person to pay attention in order to retain the information. For example, to remember a new phone number long enough to dial it requires that the numbers be held in working memory. Working memory has limited capacity, so if too many pieces of information are introduced into working memory, some of them can get lost. That is why our telephone numbers have seven digits! Trying to remember more than seven numbers at one time is difficult and confusing for most people. Little used or unnecessary information is simply discarded from working memory once it has been used. (The phone number, once dialed, is not retained.)

With time and repeated practice, information moves from working memory to long-term memory. The ideas and processes in long-term memory are more automatic because they have been practiced or repeated. For example, when learning how to read, children hold letters and then words in their short-term memory. This makes reading slow because the working memory can only hold so many pieces of information. However, as beginning readers practice, the remembering of letters and words shifts into long-term memory. This leaves more space in the working memory for sentences, paragraphs, and meaning to reside. As children gain practice in reading, the mechanics of how to do it move to long-term memory as automatic processes. These automatic processes can be called upon any time reading skills are required, no matter what the reading task is. In addition, with enough practice, anything that looks similar to reading will call up those reading skills. For example, we refer to "reading a map" not because we actually read a map in the same way we read words, but because the translation of the symbolic representation on the map is like the translation of the symbolic representation of words in reading.

As processes move to long-term memory, the relationships between them come into play. In reading, the new reader is aware of the sound each letter makes. The knowledge of what sound each letter makes moves to long-term memory and becomes automatic. With practice, the process of combining the individual sounds to make a word will move to long-term memory and allow the reader to automatically combine the letters into words. The process of combining words into sentences will also move to long-term memory eventually. It works with the previously stored processes of sounding out individual letters and individual words. When these stored processes begin to work together, they become stronger and more automatic. Associated processes and functions that work together are called "chunks." As various reading skills move to long-term memory, the parts that work together create bigger and bigger chunks. Eventually, the process of sounding out letters, recognizing words, and making sense of strings of words makes an interwoven group of processes that function together automatically so that the working memory can be used for new information. Practice stimulates the association of processes in long-term memory, making chunking automatic, too. Practice automates activities that otherwise take up a lot of working memory space and allows us to work faster.

The automation of processes happens in everything we practice. Basic math skills, if practiced, become automatic processes. Once in long-term memory, those math skills can then be called upon to help us understand chemistry or physics. Practicing the piano helps make the process of playing automatic. Once the process is automatic, moving the fingers on the keys or matching the correct key with the note on the page can be called upon when playing a new piece of music or learning to play a new instrument. Practicing a language works in much the same way. The more you practice, the more automatic it becomes. (Although we don't often notice this when learning our first language, it becomes more apparent when learning a second or third language.)

Practice seems to be a key factor in keeping automatic processes in long-term memory. Continued practice insures against forgetting. The kind of practice is also important. For example, practicing the same math problem over and over will automate the process of doing that math problem. However, if many different math problems of the same type are practiced, the idea or concept being used to do the math is what sticks in the long-term memory. Adding two plus two over and over isn't really meaningful to the process of learning math. However, if the student does enough different addition problems, she will have the more general process of addition in long-term memory to call on when it is needed. Having knowledge of how to do addition in long-term memory will be helpful when the student moves on to learning about subtraction. And both of those concepts will be called from long-term memory for other math-related applications, be they balancing a checkbook or understanding quantum mechanics.

There is some overlap in the concepts of addition and subtraction. The brain recognizes this overlap and makes connections between the two ideas. As more math skills are learned, the areas of overlap increase. This allows the brain to connect ideas and suggest similarities between ideas. The more the student knows about something, the more deeply connected the parts become. The chunks get bigger and the connections more diverse. As we practice and gain mastery of subjects, basic information becomes background—a small part of the bigger chunks that are in play in the brain. As the number of places in the brain where information is stored increase, it becomes easier to recall information and to relate it to other pieces of information.

Shifting information from working memory to long-term memory requires practice. One must practice dialing a new phone number to make it automatic. After enough practice, the recall of that series of numbers becomes automatic, and you hardly have to think about it at all. Variety in the kind of practice helps make multiple pathways to the appropriate information in the long-term memory. Children practice the alphabet until they master the twenty-six letters. They might sing an alphabet song. They might watch a television program that highlights letters. They might play a game that deals with letters. They might practice forming the letters on paper. These different ways of practicing help shift the information into the long-term memory. Using a variety of methods of practice seems to help the information stick, because it creates multiple locations for the information in the brain, making it easier to recall.

Spacing the repetition of new ideas and interleaving them with different but related information are also helpful in making the information or process stick in the long-term memory. Most children seem interested in learning about dinosaurs. If the identification of one type of dinosaur is interleaved with the identification of other types of dinosaurs, it is easier for children to recall the information about the first dinosaur later on. Learning how one type of dinosaur is different from another by interleaving the information about different types of dinosaurs helps the brain remember the types of dinosaurs and the differences between them.

Practice in recalling information strengthens the ability to find that information again when it is needed. Retrieval practice by the student (asking the student to recall information) is better than a second repetition of the information by the teacher in helping the student remember. If a student can recall information and express the information in his own words, the practice helps extract the underlying concepts and helps relate the information to other things he already knows. This strengthens the ability to recall the same information again and again and strengthens the ability to combine related concepts and information.

Finally, learning that requires effort seems to be more durable. For example, students who try to solve a problem before being given the solution learn the new information better, even if they don't get the right answer. Learning something by a method that is not your favorite makes the learning deeper because of the effort it took to learn it. The visual learner, for example, might be better off learning something literally because it requires more effort than using the method of learning favored by that student. Asking students to try to solve a new problem before they receive instruction on how to do it allows them to inspect the problem, imagine different ways of solving it, and be creative in the process. At this point they are not bound by any rules about how to solve the problem, so they can range widely for solutions, even if those solutions lie far outside the subject area. This mental exercise prepares the brain to absorb new information, even if the student does not know how to solve the problem.

TRANSFER OF LEARNING

Once a student has learned how to do addition, the ability to transfer that learning to new situations becomes important. It's good to be able to add single digits, and that is where most students begin to learn addition. When presented with addition problems containing double digits, students should be able to transfer what they know about addition to the new situation. Similarity of the processes allows the transfer to occur easily. It is easy to learn to add double-digit numbers after learning how to add single-digit numbers. When students are presented with a subtraction problem for the first time, the transfer and application of addition skills to the subtraction problem may be a little more difficult because subtraction is less similar to addition. Learning about subtraction requires some guidance and practice in order to allow the brain to create chunks linking both processes to form. Learning to translate words into mathematical operations is an even more advanced process. When students are presented with a math word problem, we want them to be able to recognize the words in the problem that are relevant to the math application, we want them to recognize the math function that is required, and we want them to apply that function to solve the problem. This is a more complex series of steps that requires the student to first read, understand, and translate words into mathematical concepts and then to interpret, understand, and apply the appropriate math concepts. The basic math skills are only a small part of the solution of the word problem, but having those math concepts in long-term memory is essential to solving the more complex problem.

In most subjects, learning is hierarchical. The basics are required before one can transfer what has been learned and apply it to more advanced ideas. If new information has not moved to long-term memory, it is difficult to apply that information to a problem. If sufficient practice has not occurred, retrieval of the information can be difficult. If basic concepts have not been linked by chunking, each process is more time consuming and hard to remember. If practice has not been varied, fewer pathways to retrieve the information have been created in the brain, making concepts harder to recall.

Once the student has learned the basics of mathematical functions, she may find the need for those functions in other subjects. In order to calculate the amounts needed to double a cookie recipe, a baker will recall basic math concepts and apply them to the baking process. In chemistry, the teacher does not usually spend time teaching mathematical processes. In order to calculate the answer to a chemistry problem, the student will need to transfer some math concepts and apply them to the chemistry problem. The ability to transfer knowledge from one situation to a new situation is sometimes problematic. The more distant the new subject is from the known subject, the harder it is for the student to make the transfer of knowledge on her own.

One way to get students to understand and attempt transfer is to tell them that it is possible. Often in school, courses on specific subjects are compartmentalized. Students in one classroom may have no idea that what they learn there might be related to or applicable in another classroom—that what they learn in history class might have some application in English class, for example. Perhaps even more relevant to students is the knowledge that what they learn in the classroom will transfer to the working world as well: "Students see a vast difference between academic and workplace information and, therefore, students perceive a low transfer between these environments."[1] Instructors can improve student learning and recall simply by telling students that what they learn in one class may be relevant in another class or in life outside the classroom.

Students may not know enough to make the connections that allow them to think about transfer. For example, when learning higher mathematics, the question in the students' minds is always "When am I ever going to use this outside this classroom?" The students may not know enough about the application of mathematics to imagine where it might be useful. It can be helpful for the instructor to give an example of a situation in which algebra or geometry or fractions might be useful in a non-classroom context or in another subject area. Making the example familiar and relevant to the student furthers the motivation for transfer.

The use of analogies can help show students how information or a skill or a concept could be useful in other contexts. An analogy presents a known concept and compares it to a new concept. The brain is always asking, how is this situation like something I already know? In instruction, providing an analogy may help to answer that question. An analogy makes the concepts easier to understand and, therefore, easier to remember. An analogy can connect new ideas to something the student already knows about. This creates a link between the two ideas, making it easier to understand and remember. The process of linking old and new ideas makes multiple connections in the brain and makes it easier to get the information back when it is needed. By giving more than one example, explaining how the skill or concept applies in those examples, and getting students to actively engage in talking about those examples, the instructor encourages the links in the brain to become much stronger, and the ability to retrieve the information or concept or skill becomes easier.

The more abstract the concept is, the more useful the analogy or example. To explain sound waves to students, a teacher might have students think about the waves created by dropping a stone into a still pond. The visual image of the waves radiating out from the place where the stone was dropped into the water can then be used as an analogy related to sound waves. Sound waves are not visible, but the ripples in a pond are. By using this analogy, the instructor links the concrete and visible example to the abstract and invisible concept. Linking the abstract concept to a concrete concept helps students make the mental connection between the two concepts. The mental picture of the expanding circles in the water helps to create an idea that can be linked to new information about sound waves and what they might look like if we could see them.

Transfer of learning is essential to everything we do. Driving a car requires transfer of learning. Creating a new computer application requires transfer of learning. Comparing World War I to the Vietnam War requires transfer of learning. Students spend a lot of time in school learning basic skills and concepts in a wide variety of subjects. If they cannot transfer what they have learned in one subject and apply it when appropriate in another subject (inside or outside the classroom), their long years of schooling are of very little value to them. Psychologist Robert Haskell puts it this way:

> In our highly complex, rapidly changing Information Age, the ability to transfer or generalize from the familiar to the less familiar, from the old to the new, not only renders our world predictable and understandable, but is a necessity for our adaptation to the technological and global demands of the 21st century.[2]

Some concepts seem to transfer almost without effort. Others seem more problematic. Concentration on conceptual rather than mechanical learning is helpful to the transfer of learning. It is not the stone hitting the water that is important in understanding sound waves. The important idea is the concept of something moving away from the center in concentric circles that will inform the student and create the bridge between actual waves and sound waves. Instructors should help students identify and learn the concepts once they have mastered the mechanical basics.

Students benefit from attempting to verbalize concepts that underlie a function. Asking students to extract underlying principles or rules that apply to new situations helps them make connections between the known and the unknown. Students who can identify how the new problem is like one they already know about achieve transfer of learning more easily. Teachers can help students transfer knowledge by asking them to describe concepts in their own words and relate the concepts to other things they already know. Asking students to verbalize these connections regularly helps create a habit of mind, which in turn helps the process of transfer.

In order to transfer learning, students must learn to reason and to apply concepts rather than simply mastering skill sets. They should be asked to practice frequent self-monitoring to assess what they know. This can be accomplished by identifying main points, rephrasing ideas in their own words, reflecting on personal experience, and self-testing. Teachers who provide instruction that emphasizes these techniques will help their students achieve understanding and assist with the transfer of learning to new ideas.

Teachers can help students discover the underlying concepts for any activity, using a variety of methods, such as testing, reflective exercises, and repeated recall. Teachers can help students accomplish deep learning and transfer of learning by giving regular and immediate feedback, especially when students give incorrect answers. Instructors should also provide students with opportunities to find the correct answers themselves. Again, this technique emphasizes the importance of allowing students to make an effort to answer a question before giving them the answer.

Professor David Billing has done research on the subject of transfer of learning. His research resulted in a number of findings about best practices that foster deep learning and transfer of learning. Among the most interesting ideas are his recommendations about the social aspects of learning.

> Transfer is promoted when learning takes place in a social context, which fosters generation of principles and explanations. Transfer improves when learning is through co-operative methods, and where there is feedback on performance with training examples.[3]

This implies that learning in a group, with a variety of opinions and viewpoints expressed, allows deeper and more resilient learning. When students learn together, their interaction helps them learn from each other. In this type of setting, transfer of learning improves. This seems to mirror the trend in library instruction over the past decade for the library instructor to be the "guide on the side," helping students make their own discoveries rather than simply telling or lecturing. It is also worth noting that employers are looking for employees who can work well in groups. Providing students with opportunities to learn to work together to find an answer to a problem is wonderful training for life after college.

INSTRUCTIONAL DESIGN

To achieve remembering and transfer, students should be presented with a variety of opportunities to practice, speculate, attempt to solve problems, recall, and compare. Instruction that provides practice in these skills must be designed carefully, understanding that a well-designed exercise will target a specific problem but also help move the student toward a conceptual understanding of the subject.

To begin designing any kind of instruction, the first question to ask is, what is the purpose of this exercise? The purpose should be stated and clear. An example would be, "This exercise is designed to teach students the standard components of an essay and in what order the components should appear." Having an exact statement about the purpose for the exercise will provide clarity for the teacher and the student. It helps everyone stay focused on the task.

The second question is closely linked to the first—what should the student learn from the exercise, lecture, class, experiment, and so on? What should the student know when she is through? In other words, what is the goal of this exercise? What are the learning outcomes I hope the students will achieve? For example,

> Learning Outcome 1: Students will name the standard components of an essay.
> Learning Outcome 2: Students will identify the standard parts of an essay.
> Learning Outcome 3: Students will map the parts of an essay in the correct sequence.

The third question is sometimes hard to answer—what do the students already know? The distance between what the students already know and what you want to teach them will determine the scope of the instruction. If the goal is to teach students how to write an essay but the students only know the alphabet, the scope of the task is quite large—probably too large to accomplish in one unit or exercise. In this case, the goal needs to be revisited and revised, or at least broken down into smaller, more manageable parts, or the instruction must happen over a long period. However, if the students know how to write sentences and paragraphs, that knowledge is probably enough preparation that teaching them how to write an essay can be accomplished in a single exercise. The scope of the task should be in keeping with the time frame available. By carefully considering what the students already know, the scope of the exercise can be adjusted if necessary.

The fourth question is, how will I convey the information to the students? It is good practice to write out the exercise as you envision it. Be specific and detail oriented.

Write out the instructions for conducting the exercise (for example, "For this exercise, students will form groups of four. Each group will need a whiteboard or flip chart and markers."). Next, estimate the amount of time it will take for students to complete the exercise. Timing can be tricky as experts often forget how much longer it takes to do something for the first time! Try out the exercise yourself or with some volunteers and see if it behaves the way you expect it to. Are the instructions clear? Does it take a longer or shorter time to complete than expected? Do you have the appropriate logistics and equipment to complete the exercise? If anything needs to be revised or rethought, start again.

The fifth question is, how will I know they learned what I wanted them to learn? What will you do to assess the learning? How will you know the students achieved the learning outcomes set for the exercise? There are many ways to assess. You might give a quiz. You might ask students to write a sample essay. You might ask the students to have a group discussion to verbalize what they learned. The assessment you choose should demonstrate the level of success for each student. The assessment is important for the students and the instructor. The assessment tells the students what they have or have not learned, and it tells the instructor whether the exercise was effective.

The sixth question is, how will I give feedback to the students? The manner of providing feedback often depends on the method of assessment. If students hand in a written essay, the instructor can give feedback in writing on the essay itself. Or the instructor could have a face-to-face conversation with each student. Or the instructor could give feedback during a group discussion. For information literacy instruction, feedback is essential. If students leave their instruction session without feedback and correction (if necessary), there may not be another opportunity for the librarian to connect with those students. If they leave the session without knowing how well they learned, or what they did not learn, the time they spent in the class was not well spent.

The final question is, will students receive a grade on this exercise and, if so, what will the grade be based on? A grade is often part of the feedback an instructor can offer to a student. It might be a simple checkmark to show that the student completed the work. It might be a letter grade to show the quality of the student's work. If a grade will be awarded, the student should know what the grade was based on. The best way to convey this information is to create a grading rubric that addresses the learning outcomes for the exercise.

In information literacy it is not always easy to know what students already know, simply because information literacy instruction is often a one-time teaching event. The librarian does not have the benefit of working with students over the course of a semester and does not often participate in the class itself. That means the librarian must rely on the instructor of the class to gauge what the students know or must base instruction on assumptions about what students taking this class might know. Librarians with many years of experience can estimate fairly closely what students of a specific level might know, but for less seasoned librarians, this task can be difficult. Working with faculty to understand what students in their classes know and what they want their students to learn will help the instruction librarian create a relevant and useful class for students.

How do we know that students have learned what we wanted them to learn? Assessment is a standard part of most instruction. The assessment is a measure of student learning, based on the learning outcomes set for the task. Assessments can take many forms—tests, written comments, class discussions, presentations, and so on. Evaluating assessments objectively is not always easy. To make evaluation as objective as possible, instructors often use a grading or assessment rubric. Use of a rubric allows instructors to quantify, to some extent, the quality of the results of the assessment.

WHAT IS A RUBRIC?

A rubric is an assessment tool that allows objective grading of student performance. The rubric will list the parts of the student's performance that are to be evaluated (the learning outcomes) and the level of achievement possible (how the grading scale works) along with a score for each outcome component and a final total score (how well did the student show that she achieved the learning objectives for the exercise?). For example:

> Learning Outcome/Objective 1: Students will name the standard components of an essay.
> Learning Outcome/Objective 2: Students will identify the standard parts of an essay.
> Learning Outcome/Objective 3: Students will map the parts of an essay in the correct sequence.

This information can be put in a chart format for ease of grading:

> 4 points: Excellent
> 3 points: Good
> 2 points: Needs Work
> 1 point: Unsatisfactory
> 0 points: Unsatisfactory

	4 parts	3 parts	2 parts	1 part	No parts
Learning Outcome/Objective 1: Students will name the standard components of an essay.					
Learning Outcome/Objective 2: Students will identify the standard parts of an essay.					
Learning Outcome/Objective 3: Students will map the parts of an essay in the correct sequence.					

Receiving the rubric before the assessment begins allows students to understand what the exercise entails and lets them know what they need to do to successfully complete the exercise. Once the exercise is completed, the rubric is used to assign points for each objective based on each student's performance. Points are then totaled and a grade assigned based on the instructor's benchmark for success. The grade could be a number of points or a letter, or it could be a designation of the quality of the work—excellent, fair, poor, and so on.

The rubric helps students understand where their learning is lacking as well as where they have been successful. It is important to construct a rubric that targets the learning outcomes and matches them to the students' performance on the assessment. The rubric will also tell the instructor where the exercise may be lacking. If all students do poorly on one part of the assessment, it may indicate that the exercise needs to be revised or that the topic of that part of the assessment needs more time and attention during class.

A well-designed exercise will tell students the purpose for the exercise. They should know the learning outcomes for the exercise. They should know how their learning will be assessed, and they should know how they will be graded. They should be given the materials and time needed to accomplish the task, along with explicit instructions about how to complete the exercise. They should be given feedback on their level of success, preferably while the assessment is still fresh in their minds. If possible, giving the students an opportunity to revise and resubmit in areas where they did not do well will serve to strengthen their skills.

An important part of instructional design that is often assumed rather than explicit occurs on the instructor's side of the equation. The instructor should assess the success of the exercise, based on the students' performance, and revise it if necessary. If the students did not have the time or materials needed to complete the task, the instructor should revise the exercise to include more time, plan for the provision of materials, or rethink the logistics of the exercise. If the students did not do well in meeting the learning outcomes, the instructor should identify the reasons for the poor result and revise the exercise accordingly, adjusting the scope as needed. For example, if 50 percent of the students did not include a conclusion as the final part of an essay, the section of the exercise that attempted to teach the students about writing a conclusion probably needs to be revised. Assessments and learning outcomes need to be compared and revised regularly to ensure that the students can succeed.

An instructor may create a series of exercises in which the skills learned in previous classes are applied to the next exercise in the series, creating a scaffold of increasingly challenging exercises. This scaffolding of learning allows students to recall, to practice, to apply what they learned in previous exercises to new situations, to analogize, to conceptualize, and to transfer knowledge. In progressing from a novice level in information literacy to an expert level in information literacy, as in most learning, students begin with basics and build on those basics as they gain experience and knowledge.

NOTES ————————————————————————————————

1. Daniel T. Willingham, *Why Don't Students Like School?* (San Francisco: Jossey-Bass, 2009), 244.

2. Robert E. Haskell, *Transfer of Learning: Cognition, Instruction, and Reasoning* (New York: Academic Press, 2001), 37.

3. David Billing, "Teaching for Transfer of Core/Key Skills in Higher Education: Cognitive Skills," *Higher Education* 53 (2007): 483.

The ACRL Framework for Information Literacy for Higher Education

INTRODUCTION

This *Framework for Information Literacy for Higher Education* (*Framework*) grows out of a belief that information literacy as an educational reform movement will realize its potential only through a richer, more complex set of core ideas. During the fifteen years since the publication of the *Information Literacy Competency Standards for Higher Education*,[1] academic librarians and their partners in higher education associations have developed learning outcomes, tools, and resources that some institutions have deployed to infuse information literacy concepts and skills into their curricula. However, the rapidly changing higher education environment, along with the dynamic and often uncertain information ecosystem in which all of us work and live, require new attention to be focused on foundational ideas about that ecosystem. Students have a greater role and responsibility in creating new knowledge, in understanding the contours and the changing dynamics of the world of information, and in using information, data, and scholarship ethically. Teaching faculty have a greater responsibility in designing curricula and assignments that foster enhanced engagement with the core ideas about information and scholarship within their disciplines. Librarians have a greater responsibility in identifying core ideas within their own knowledge domain that can extend learning for students, in creating a new cohesive curriculum for information literacy, and in collaborating more extensively with faculty.

The *Framework* offered here is called a framework intentionally because it is based on a cluster of interconnected core concepts, with flexible options for implementation, rather than on a set of standards or learning outcomes, or any prescriptive enumeration of skills. At the heart of this *Framework* are conceptual understandings that organize many other concepts and ideas about information, research, and scholarship into a coherent whole. These conceptual understandings are informed by the work of Wiggins and McTighe,[2] which focuses on essential concepts and questions in developing curricula, and also by *threshold concepts*,[3] which are those ideas in any discipline that are passageways or portals to enlarged understanding or ways of thinking and practicing within that discipline. This *Framework* draws upon an ongoing Delphi Study that has identified several threshold concepts in information literacy,[4] but the *Framework* has been molded using fresh ideas and emphases for the threshold concepts. Two added elements illustrate important learning goals related to those concepts: *knowledge practices*,[5] which are demonstrations of ways in which learners can increase their understanding of these information literacy concepts, and *dispositions*,[6] which describe ways in which to address the affective, attitudinal, or valuing dimension of learning. The *Framework* is organized into six frames, each consisting of a concept central to information literacy, a set of knowledge practices, and a set of dispositions. The six concepts that anchor the frames are presented alphabetically:

- Authority Is Constructed and Contextual
- Information Creation as a Process
- Information Has Value
- Research as Inquiry
- Scholarship as Conversation
- Searching as Strategic Exploration

Neither the knowledge practices nor the dispositions that support each concept are intended to prescribe what local institutions should do in using the *Framework*; each library and its partners on campus will need to deploy these frames to best fit their own situation, including designing learning outcomes. For the same reason, these lists should not be considered exhaustive.

In addition, this *Framework* draws significantly upon the concept of metaliteracy,[7] which offers a renewed vision of information literacy as an overarching set of abilities in which students are consumers and creators of information who can participate successfully in collaborative spaces.[8] Metaliteracy demands behavioral, affective, cognitive, and metacognitive engagement with the information ecosystem.

This *Framework* depends on these core ideas of metaliteracy, with special focus on metacognition,[9] or critical self-reflection, as crucial to becoming more self-directed in that rapidly changing ecosystem.

Because this *Framework* envisions information literacy as extending the arc of learning throughout students' academic careers and as converging with other academic and social learning goals, an expanded definition of information literacy is offered here to emphasize dynamism, flexibility, individual growth, and community learning:

> Information literacy is the set of integrated abilities encompassing the reflective discovery of information, the understanding of how information is produced and valued, and the use of information in creating new knowledge and participating ethically in communities of learning.

The *Framework* opens the way for librarians, faculty, and other institutional partners to redesign instruction sessions, assignments, courses, and even curricula; to connect information literacy with student success initiatives; to collaborate on pedagogical research and involve students themselves in that research; and to create wider conversations about student learning, the scholarship of teaching and learning, and the assessment of learning on local campuses and beyond.

NOTES

1. Association of College & Research Libraries, *Information Literacy Competency Standards for Higher Education* (Chicago, 2000).

2. Grant Wiggins and Jay McTighe. *Understanding by Design.* (Alexandria, VA: Association for Supervision and Curriculum Development, 2004).

3. Threshold concepts are core or foundational concepts that, once grasped by the learner, create new perspectives and ways of understanding a discipline or challenging knowledge domain. Such concepts produce transformation within the learner; without them, the learner does not acquire expertise in that field of knowledge. Threshold concepts can be thought of as portals through which the learner must pass in order to develop new perspectives and wider understanding. Jan H. F. Meyer, Ray Land, and Caroline Baillie. "Editors' Preface." In *Threshold Concepts and Transformational Learning*, edited by Jan H. F. Meyer, Ray Land, and Caroline Baillie, ix–xlii. (Rotterdam, Netherlands: Sense Publishers, 2010).

4. For information on this unpublished, in-progress Delphi Study on threshold concepts and information literacy, conducted by Lori Townsend, Amy Hofer, Silvia Lu, and Korey Brunetti, see www.ilthresholdconcepts.com. Lori Townsend, Korey Brunetti, and Amy R. Hofer. "Threshold Concepts and Information Literacy." *portal: Libraries and the Academy* 11, no. 3 (2011): 853–69.

5. Knowledge practices are the proficiencies or abilities that learners develop as a result of their comprehending a threshold concept.

6. Generally, a disposition is a tendency to act or think in a particular way. More specifically, a disposition is a cluster of preferences, attitudes, and intentions, as well as a set of capabilities that allow the preferences to become realized in a particular way. Gavriel Salomon. "To Be or Not to Be (Mindful)." Paper presented at the American Educational Research Association Meetings, New Orleans, LA, 1994.

7. Metaliteracy expands the scope of traditional information skills (determine, access, locate, understand, produce, and use information) to include the collaborative production and sharing of information in participatory digital environments (collaborate,

produce, and share). This approach requires an ongoing adaptation to emerging technologies and an understanding of the critical thinking and reflection required to engage in these spaces as producers, collaborators, and distributors. Thomas P. Mackey and Trudi E. Jacobson. *Metaliteracy: Reinventing Information Literacy to Empower Learners.* (Chicago: Neal-Schuman, 2014).

8. Thomas P. Mackey and Trudi E. Jacobson. "Reframing Information Literacy as a Metaliteracy." *College and Research Libraries* 72, no. 1 (2011): 62–78.

9. Metacognition is an awareness and understanding of one's own thought processes. It focuses on how people learn and process information, taking into consideration people's awareness of how they learn. (Jennifer A. Livingston. "Metacognition: An Overview." Online paper, State University of New York at Buffalo, Graduate School of Education, 1997. http://gse.buffalo.edu/fas/shuell/cep564/metacog.htm.)

AUTHORITY IS CONSTRUCTED AND CONTEXTUAL

Information resources reflect their creators' expertise and credibility, and are evaluated based on the information need and the context in which the information will be used. Authority is constructed in that various communities may recognize different types of authority. It is contextual in that the information need may help to determine the level of authority required.

Experts understand that authority is a type of influence recognized or exerted within a community. Experts view authority with an attitude of informed skepticism and an openness to new perspectives, additional voices, and changes in schools of thought. Experts understand the need to determine the validity of the information created by different authorities and to acknowledge biases that privilege some sources of authority over others, especially in terms of others' worldviews, gender, sexual orientation, and cultural orientations. An understanding of this concept enables novice learners to critically examine all evidence—be it a short blog post or a peer-reviewed conference proceeding—and to ask relevant questions about origins, context, and suitability for the current information need. Thus, novice learners come to respect the expertise that authority represents while remaining skeptical of the systems that have elevated that authority and the information created by it. Experts know how to seek authoritative voices but also recognize that unlikely voices can be authoritative, depending on need. Novice learners may need to rely on basic indicators of authority, such as type of publication or author credentials, where experts recognize schools of thought or discipline-specific paradigms.

Knowledge Practices

Learners who are developing their information literate abilities

- define different types of authority, such as subject expertise (e.g., scholarship), societal position (e.g., public office or title), or special experience (e.g., participating in a historic event);
- use research tools and indicators of authority to determine the credibility of sources, understanding the elements that might temper this credibility;
- understand that many disciplines have acknowledged authorities in the sense of well-known scholars and publications that are widely considered "standard," and yet, even in those situations, some scholars would challenge the authority of those sources;
- recognize that authoritative content may be packaged formally or informally and may include sources of all media types;
- acknowledge they are developing their own authoritative voices in a particular area and recognize the responsibilities this entails, including seeking accuracy and reliability, respecting intellectual property, and participating in communities of practice; and
- understand the increasingly social nature of the information ecosystem where authorities actively connect with one another and sources develop over time.

Dispositions

Learners who are developing their information literate abilities

- develop and maintain an open mind when encountering varied and sometimes conflicting perspectives;
- motivate themselves to find authoritative sources, recognizing that authority may be conferred or manifested in unexpected ways;
- develop awareness of the importance of assessing content with a skeptical stance and with a self-awareness of their own biases and worldview;
- question traditional notions of granting authority and recognize the value of diverse ideas and worldviews; and
- are conscious that maintaining these attitudes and actions requires frequent self-evaluation.

INFORMATION CREATION AS A PROCESS

Information in any format is produced to convey a message and is shared via a selected delivery method. The iterative processes of researching, creating, revising, and disseminating information vary, and the resulting product reflects these differences.

The information creation process could result in a range of information formats and modes of delivery, so experts look beyond format when selecting resources to use. The unique capabilities and constraints of each creation process as well as the specific information needed determine how the product is used. Experts recognize that information creations are valued differently in different contexts, such as academia or the workplace. Elements that affect or reflect on the creation, such as a pre- or post-publication editing or reviewing process, may be indicators of quality. The dynamic nature of information creation and dissemination requires ongoing attention to understand evolving creation processes. Recognizing the nature of information creation, experts look to the underlying processes of creation as well as the final product to critically evaluate the usefulness of the information. Novice learners begin to recognize the significance of the creation process, leading them to increasingly sophisticated choices when matching information products with their information needs.

Knowledge Practices

Learners who are developing their information literate abilities

- articulate the capabilities and constraints of information developed through various creation processes;
- assess the fit between an information product's creation process and a particular information need;
- articulate the traditional and emerging processes of information creation and dissemination in a particular discipline;
- recognize that information may be perceived differently based on the format in which it is packaged;
- recognize the implications of information formats that contain static or dynamic information;
- monitor the value that is placed upon different types of information products in varying contexts;
- transfer knowledge of capabilities and constraints to new types of information products; and
- develop, in their own creation processes, an understanding that their choices impact the purposes for which the information product will be used and the message it conveys.

Dispositions

Learners who are developing their information literate abilities

- are inclined to seek out characteristics of information products that indicate the underlying creation process;
- value the process of matching an information need with an appropriate product;
- accept that the creation of information may begin initially through communicating in a range of formats or modes;
- accept the ambiguity surrounding the potential value of information creation expressed in emerging formats or modes;
- resist the tendency to equate format with the underlying creation process; and
- understand that different methods of information dissemination with different purposes are available for their use.

INFORMATION HAS VALUE

Information possesses several dimensions of value, including as a commodity, as a means of education, as a means to influence, and as a means of negotiating and understanding the world. Legal and socioeconomic interests influence information production and dissemination.

The value of information is manifested in various contexts, including publishing practices, access to information, the commodification of personal information, and intellectual property laws. The novice learner may struggle to understand the diverse values of information in an environment where "free" information and related services are plentiful and the concept of intellectual property is first encountered through rules of citation or warnings about plagiarism and copyright law. As creators and users of information, experts understand their rights and responsibilities when participating in a community of scholarship. Experts understand that value may be wielded by powerful interests in ways that marginalize certain voices. However, value may also be leveraged by individuals and organizations to effect change and for civic, economic, social, or personal gains. Experts also understand that the individual is responsible for making deliberate and informed choices about when to comply with and when to contest current legal and socioeconomic practices concerning the value of information.

Knowledge Practices

Learners who are developing their information literate abilities

- give credit to the original ideas of others through proper attribution and citation;
- understand that intellectual property is a legal and social construct that varies by culture;

- articulate the purpose and distinguishing characteristics of copyright, fair use, open access, and the public domain;
- understand how and why some individuals or groups of individuals may be underrepresented or systematically marginalized within the systems that produce and disseminate information;
- recognize issues of access or lack of access to information sources;
- decide where and how their information is published;
- understand how the commodification of their personal information and online interactions affects the information they receive and the information they produce or disseminate online; and
- make informed choices regarding their online actions in full awareness of issues related to privacy and the commodification of personal information.

Dispositions

Learners who are developing their information literate abilities

- respect the original ideas of others;
- value the skills, time, and effort needed to produce knowledge;
- see themselves as contributors to the information marketplace rather than only consumers of it; and
- are inclined to examine their own information privilege.

RESEARCH AS INQUIRY

Research is iterative and depends upon asking increasingly complex or new questions whose answers in turn develop additional questions or lines of inquiry in any field.

Experts see inquiry as a process that focuses on problems or questions in a discipline or between disciplines that are open or unresolved. Experts recognize the collaborative effort within a discipline to extend the knowledge in that field. Many times, this process includes points of disagreement where debate and dialogue work to deepen the conversations around knowledge. This process of inquiry extends beyond the academic world to the community at large, and the process of inquiry may focus upon personal, professional, or societal needs. The spectrum of inquiry ranges from asking simple questions that depend upon basic recapitulation of knowledge to increasingly sophisticated abilities to refine research questions, use more advanced research methods, and explore more diverse disciplinary perspectives. Novice learners acquire strategic perspectives on inquiry and a greater repertoire of investigative methods.

Knowledge Practices

Learners who are developing their information literate abilities

- formulate questions for research based on information gaps or on reexamination of existing, possibly conflicting, information;
- determine an appropriate scope of investigation;
- deal with complex research by breaking complex questions into simple ones, limiting the scope of investigations;
- use various research methods, based on need, circumstance, and type of inquiry;
- monitor gathered information and assess for gaps or weaknesses;
- organize information in meaningful ways;
- synthesize ideas gathered from multiple sources; and
- draw reasonable conclusions based on the analysis and interpretation of information.

Dispositions

Learners who are developing their information literate abilities

- consider research as open-ended exploration and engagement with information;
- appreciate that a question may appear to be simple but still disruptive and important to research;
- value intellectual curiosity in developing questions and learning new investigative methods;
- maintain an open mind and a critical stance;
- value persistence, adaptability, and flexibility and recognize that ambiguity can benefit the research process;
- seek multiple perspectives during information gathering and assessment;
- seek appropriate help when needed;
- follow ethical and legal guidelines in gathering and using information; and
- demonstrate intellectual humility (i.e., recognize their own intellectual or experiential limitations).

SCHOLARSHIP AS CONVERSATION

Communities of scholars, researchers, or professionals engage in sustained discourse with new insights and discoveries occurring over time as a result of varied perspectives and interpretations.

Research in scholarly and professional fields is a discursive practice in which ideas are formulated, debated, and weighed against one another over extended periods of time. Instead of seeking discrete answers to complex problems, experts understand that a given issue may be characterized by several competing perspectives as part of an ongoing conversation in which information users and creators come together and negotiate meaning. Experts understand that, while some topics have established answers through this process, a query may not have a single uncontested answer. Experts are therefore inclined to seek out many perspectives, not merely the ones with which they are familiar. These perspectives might be in their own discipline or profession or may be in other fields. While novice learners and experts at all levels can take part in the conversation, established power and authority structures may influence their ability to participate and can privilege certain voices and information. Developing familiarity with the sources of evidence, methods, and modes of discourse in the field assists novice learners to enter the conversation. New forms of scholarly and research conversations provide more avenues in which a wide variety of individuals may have a voice in the conversation. Providing attribution to relevant previous research is also an obligation of participation in the conversation. It enables the conversation to move forward and strengthens one's voice in the conversation.

Knowledge Practices

Learners who are developing their information literate abilities

- cite the contributing work of others in their own information production;
- contribute to scholarly conversation at an appropriate level, such as local online community, guided discussion, undergraduate research journal, conference presentation/poster session;
- identify barriers to entering scholarly conversation via various venues;
- critically evaluate contributions made by others in participatory information environments;
- identify the contribution that particular articles, books, and other scholarly pieces make to disciplinary knowledge;
- summarize the changes in scholarly perspective over time on a particular topic within a specific discipline; and
- recognize that a given scholarly work may not represent the only - or even the majority - perspective on the issue.

Dispositions

Learners who are developing their information literate abilities

- recognize they are often entering into an ongoing scholarly conversation and not a finished conversation;
- seek out conversations taking place in their research area;
- see themselves as contributors to scholarship rather than only consumers of it;
- recognize that scholarly conversations take place in various venues;

- suspend judgment on the value of a particular piece of scholarship until the larger context for the scholarly conversation is better understood;
- understand the responsibility that comes with entering the conversation through participatory channels;
- value user-generated content and evaluate contributions made by others; and
- recognize that systems privilege authorities and that not having a fluency in the language and process of a discipline disempowers their ability to participate and engage.

SEARCHING AS STRATEGIC EXPLORATION

Searching for information is often nonlinear and iterative, requiring the evaluation of a range of information sources and the mental flexibility to pursue alternate avenues as new understanding develops.

The act of searching often begins with a question that directs the act of finding needed information. Encompassing inquiry, discovery, and serendipity, searching identifies both possible relevant sources as well as the means to access those sources. Experts realize that information searching is a contextualized, complex experience that affects, and is affected by, the cognitive, affective, and social dimensions of the searcher. Novice learners may search a limited set of resources, while experts may search more broadly and deeply to determine the most appropriate information within the project scope. Likewise, novice learners tend to use few search strategies, while experts select from various search strategies, depending on the sources, scope, and context of the information need.

Knowledge Practices

Learners who are developing their information literate abilities

- determine the initial scope of the task required to meet their information needs;
- identify interested parties, such as scholars, organizations, governments, and industries, who might produce information about a topic and then determine how to access that information;
- utilize divergent (e.g., brainstorming) and convergent (e.g., selecting the best source) thinking when searching;
- match information needs and search strategies to appropriate search tools;
- design and refine needs and search strategies as necessary, based on search results;
- understand how information systems (i.e., collections of recorded information) are organized in order to access relevant information;

- use different types of searching language (e.g., controlled vocabulary, keywords, natural language) appropriately; and
- manage searching processes and results effectively.

Dispositions

Learners who are developing their information literate abilities

- exhibit mental flexibility and creativity;
- understand that first attempts at searching do not always produce adequate results;
- realize that information sources vary greatly in content and format and have varying relevance and value, depending on the needs and nature of the search;
- seek guidance from experts, such as librarians, researchers, and professionals;
- recognize the value of browsing and other serendipitous methods of information gathering; and
- persist in the face of search challenges, and know when they have enough information to complete the information task.

APPENDIX 1: IMPLEMENTING THE FRAMEWORK

Suggestions on How to Use the Framework for Information Literacy for Higher Education

The *Framework* is a mechanism for guiding the development of information literacy programs within higher education institutions while also promoting discussion about the nature of key concepts in information in general education and disciplinary studies. The *Framework* encourages thinking about how librarians, faculty, and others can address core or portal concepts and associated elements in the information field within the context of higher education. The *Framework* will help librarians contextualize and integrate information literacy for their institutions and will encourage a deeper understanding of what knowledge practices and dispositions an information literate student should develop. The *Framework* redefines the boundaries of what librarians teach and how they conceptualize the study of information within the curricula of higher education institutions.

The *Framework* has been conceived as a set of living documents on which the profession will build. The key product is a set of frames, or lenses, through which to view information literacy, each of which includes a concept central to information literacy, knowledge practices, and dispositions. The Association of College & Research Libraries (ACRL) encourages the library community to discuss the new *Framework* widely and to develop resources such as curriculum guides, concept maps, and assessment instruments to supplement the core set of materials in the frames.

As a first step, ACRL encourages librarians to read through the entire *Framework* and discuss the implications of this new approach for the information literacy program at their institution. Possibilities include convening a discussion among librarians at an institution or joining an online discussion of librarians. In addition, as one becomes familiar with the frames, consider discussing them with professionals in the institution's center for teaching and learning, office of undergraduate education, or similar departments to see whether some synergies exist between this approach and other institutional curricular initiatives.

The frames can guide the redesign of information literacy programs for general education courses, for upper level courses in students' major departments, and for graduate student education. The frames are intended to demonstrate the contrast in thinking between *novice learner* and *expert* in a specific area; movement may take place over the course of a student's academic career. Mapping out in what way specific concepts will be integrated into specific curriculum levels is one of the challenges of implementing the *Framework*. ACRL encourages librarians to work with faculty, departmental or college curriculum committees, instructional designers, staff from centers for teaching and learning, and others to design information literacy programs in a holistic way.

ACRL realizes that many information literacy librarians currently meet with students via one-shot classes, especially in introductory level classes. Over the course of a student's academic program, one-shot sessions that address a particular need at a particular time, systematically integrated into the curriculum, can play a significant role in an information literacy program. It is important for librarians and teaching faculty to understand that the *Framework* is not designed to be implemented in a single information literacy session in a student's academic career; it is intended to be developmentally and systematically integrated into the student's academic program at variety of levels. This may take considerable time to implement fully in many institutions.

ACRL encourages information literacy librarians to be imaginative and innovative in implementing the *Framework* in their institution. The *Framework* is not intended to be prescriptive but to be used as a guidance document in shaping an institutional program. ACRL recommends piloting the implementation of the *Framework* in a context that is useful to a specific institution, assessing the results and sharing experiences with colleagues.

HOW TO USE THIS FRAMEWORK

- Read and reflect on the entire *Framework* document.
- Convene or join a group of librarians to discuss the implications of this approach to information literacy for your institution.
- Reach out to potential partners in your institution, such as departmental curriculum committees, centers for teaching and learning, or offices of undergraduate or graduate studies, to discuss how to implement the *Framework* in your institutional context.

- Using the *Framework*, pilot the development of information literacy sessions within a particular academic program in your institution, and assess and share the results with your colleagues.
- Share instructional materials with other information literacy librarians in the online repository developed by ACRL.

Introduction for Faculty and Administrators

CONSIDERING INFORMATION LITERACY

Information literacy is the set of integrated abilities encompassing the reflective discovery of information, the understanding of how information is produced and valued, and the use of information in creating new knowledge and participating ethically in communities of learning.

This *Framework* sets forth these information literacy concepts and describes how librarians as information professionals can facilitate the development of information literacy by postsecondary students.

CREATING A FRAMEWORK

ACRL has played a leading role in promoting information literacy in higher education for decades. The *Information Literacy Competency Standards for Higher Education* (*Standards*), first published in 2000, enabled colleges and universities to position information literacy as an essential learning outcome in the curriculum and promoted linkages with general education programs, service learning, problem-based learning, and other pedagogies focused on deeper learning. Regional accrediting bodies, the American Association of Colleges and Universities (AAC&U), and various discipline-specific organizations employed and adapted the *Standards*.

It is time for a fresh look at information literacy, especially in light of changes in higher education, coupled with increasingly complex information ecosystems. To that end, an ACRL Task Force developed the *Framework*. The *Framework* seeks to address the great potential for information literacy as a deeper, more integrated learning agenda, addressing academic and technical courses, undergraduate research, community-based learning, and co-curricular learning experiences of entering freshman through graduation. The *Framework* focuses attention on the vital role of collaboration and its potential for increasing student understanding of the processes of knowledge creation and scholarship. The *Framework* also emphasizes student participation and creativity, highlighting the importance of these contributions.

The *Framework* is developed around a set of "frames," which are those critical gateway or portal concepts through which students must pass to develop genuine expertise within a discipline, profession, or knowledge domain. Each frame includes a knowledge practices section used to demonstrate how the mastery of the concept leads to application in new situations and knowledge generation. Each frame also includes a set of dispositions that address the affective areas of learning.

For Faculty: How to Use the Framework

A vital benefit in using threshold concepts as one of the underpinnings for the *Framework* is the potential for collaboration among disciplinary faculty, librarians, teaching and learning center staff, and others. Creating a community of conversations about this enlarged understanding should engender more collaboration, more innovative course designs, and a more inclusive consideration of learning within and beyond the classroom. Threshold concepts originated as faculty pedagogical research within disciplines. Because information literacy is both a disciplinary and a transdisciplinary learning agenda, using a conceptual framework for information literacy program planning, librarian-faculty collaboration, and student co-curricular projects can offer great potential for curricular enrichment and transformation. As a faculty member, you can take the following approaches:

- Investigate threshold concepts in your discipline and gain an understanding of the approach used in the *Framework* as it applies to the discipline you know.
  - What are the specialized information skills in your discipline that students should develop, such as using primary sources (history) or accessing and managing large data sets (science)?

- Look for workshops at your campus teaching and learning center on the flipped classroom and consider how such practices could be incorporated into your courses.
  - What information and research assignments can students do outside of class to arrive prepared to apply concepts and conduct collaborative projects?

- Partner with your IT department and librarians to develop new kinds of multimedia assignments for courses.
  - What kinds of workshops and other services should be available for students involved in multimedia design and production?

- Help students view themselves as information producers, individually and collaboratively.
  - In your program, how do students interact with, evaluate, produce, and share information in various formats and modes?

- Consider the knowledge practices and dispositions in each information literacy frame for possible integration into your own courses and academic program.
  - How might you and a librarian design learning experiences and assignments that will encourage students to assess their own attitudes, strengths/weaknesses, and knowledge gaps related to information?

For Administrators: How to Support the Framework

Through reading the *Framework* document and discussing it with your institutions' librarians, you can begin to focus on the best mechanisms to implement the *Framework* in your institution. As an administrator, you can take the following approaches:

- Host or encourage a series of campus conversations about how the institution can incorporate the *Framework* into student learning outcomes and supporting curriculum.
- Provide the resources to enhance faculty expertise and opportunities for understanding and incorporating the *Framework* into the curriculum.
- Encourage committees working on planning documents related to teaching and learning (at the department, program, and institutional levels) to include concepts from the *Framework* in their work.
- Provide resources to support a meaningful assessment of information literacy of students at various levels at your institution.
- Promote partnerships between faculty, librarians, instructional designers, and others to develop meaningful ways for students to become content creators, especially in their disciplines.

APPENDIX 2:
BACKGROUND OF THE FRAMEWORK DEVELOPMENT

The *Information Literacy Competency Standards for Higher Education* were published in 2000 and brought information literacy into higher education conversations and advanced our field. These, like all ACRL standards, are reviewed cyclically. In July 2011, ACRL appointed a Task Force to decide what, if anything, to do with the current *Standards*. In June 2012, that Task Force recommended that the current *Standards* be significantly revised. This previous review Task Force made recommendations that informed the current revision Task Force, formed in 2013, with the following charge:

> to update the *Information Literacy Competency Standards for Higher Education* so they reflect the current thinking on such things as the creation and dissemination of knowledge, the changing global higher education and learning environment, the shift from information literacy to information fluency, and the expanding definition of information literacy to include multiple literacies, for example, transliteracy, media literacy, digital literacy, etc.

The Task Force released the first version of the *Framework* in two parts in February and April of 2014 and received comments via two online hearings and a feedback form available online for four weeks. The committee then revised the document, released the second draft on June 17, 2014, and sought extensive feedback through a feedback form, two online hearings, an in-person hearing, and analysis of social media and topical blog posts.

On a regular basis, the Task Force used all of ACRL's and American Library Association's (ALA) communication channels to reach individual members and ALA and ACRL units (committees, sections, round tables, ethnic caucuses, chapters, and divisions) with updates. The Task Force's liaison at ACRL maintained a private e-mail distribution list of over 1,300 individuals who attended a fall, spring, or summer online forum; provided comments to the February, April, June, or November drafts; or were otherwise identified as having strong interest and expertise. This included members of the Task Force that drafted the *Standards*, leading Library Information Science (LIS) researchers and national project directors, members of the Information Literacy Rubric Development Team for the Association of American Colleges & Universities, and Valid Assessment of Learning in Undergraduate Education initiative. Via all these channels, the Task Force regularly shared updates, invited discussion at virtual and in-person forums and hearings, and encouraged comments on public drafts of the proposed *Framework*.

ACRL recognized early on that the effect of any changes to the *Standards* would be significant both within the library profession and in higher education more broadly. In addition to general announcements, the Task Force contacted nearly 60 researchers who cited the *Standards* in publications outside LIS literature, more than 70 deans, associate deans, directors or chairs of LIS schools, and invited specific staff leaders (and press or communications contacts) at more than 70 other higher education associations, accrediting agencies, and library associations and consortia to encourage their members to read and comment on the draft.

The Task Force systematically reviewed feedback from the first and second drafts of the *Framework*, including comments, criticism, and praise provided through formal and informal channels. The three official online feedback forms had 562 responses; numerous direct e-mails were sent to members of the Task Force. The group was proactive in tracking feedback on social media, namely blog posts and Twitter. While the data harvested from social media are not exhaustive, the Task Force made its best efforts to include all known Twitter conversations, blog posts, and blog commentary. In total, there were several hundred feedback documents, totaling over a thousand pages, under review. The content of these documents was analyzed by members of the Task Force and coded using HyperResearch, a qualitative data analysis software. During the drafting and vetting process, the Task Force provided more detail on the feedback analysis in an online FAQ document.

The Task Force continued to revise the document and published the third revision in November 2014, again announcing broadly and seeking comments via a feedback form.

As of November 2014, the Task Force members included the following:

- Craig Gibson, Professor, Ohio State University Libraries (Co-chair)
- Trudi E. Jacobson, Distinguished Librarian and Head, Information Literacy Department, University at Albany, SUNY, University Libraries (Co-chair)
- Elizabeth Berman, Science and Engineering Librarian, University of Vermont (Member)
- Carl O. DiNardo, Assistant Professor and Coordinator of Library Instruction/ Science Librarian, Eckerd College (Member)
- Lesley S. J. Farmer, Professor, California State University–Long Beach (Member)
- Ellie A. Fogarty, Vice President, Middle States Commission on Higher Education (Member)
- Diane M. Fulkerson, Social Sciences and Education Librarian, University of South Florida in Lakeland (Member)
- Merinda Kaye Hensley, Instructional Services Librarian and Scholarly Commons Co-coordinator, University of Illinois at Urbana-Champaign (Member)
- Joan K. Lippincott, Associate Executive Director, Coalition for Networked Information (Member)
- Michelle S. Millet, Library Director, John Carroll University (Member)
- Troy Swanson, Teaching and Learning Librarian, Moraine Valley Community College (Member)
- Lori Townsend, Data Librarian for Social Sciences and Humanities, University of New Mexico (Member)
- Julie Ann Garrison, Associate Dean of Research and Instructional Services, Grand Valley State University (Board Liaison)
- Kate Ganski, Library Instruction Coordinator, University of Wisconsin–Milwaukee (Visiting Program Officer, from September 1, 2013, through June 30, 2014)
- Kara Malenfant, Senior Strategist for Special Initiatives, Association of College and Research Libraries (Staff Liaison)

In December 2014, the Task Force made final changes. Two other ACRL groups reviewed and provided feedback on the final drafts: the ACRL Information Literacy Standards Committee and the ACRL Standards Committee. The latter group submitted the final document and recommendations to the ACRL Board for its review at the 2015 ALA Midwinter Meeting in Chicago.

> *Note:* On February 2, 2015, at the 2015 ALA Midwinter Meeting, the ACRL Board took the official action of 'filing' the *Framework* document, in accordance with parliamentary procedure. This allows it to be changed without needing Board approval, in order to foster its intended flexibility and development.

APPENDIX 3: SOURCES FOR FURTHER READING

The following sources are suggested readings for those who want to learn more about the ideas underpinning the *Framework*, especially the use of threshold concepts and related pedagogical models. Some readings here also explore other models for information literacy, discuss students' challenges with information literacy, or offer examples of assessment of threshold concepts. Landmark works on threshold concept theory and research on this list are the edited volumes by Meyer, Land, and Baillie (*Threshold Concepts and Transformational Learning*) and by Meyer and Land (*Threshold Concepts and Troublesome Knowledge: Linkages to Ways of Thinking and Practicing within the Disciplines*). In addition, numerous research articles, conference papers, reports, and presentations on threshold concepts are cited on the regularly updated website Threshold Concepts: Undergraduate Teaching, Postgraduate Training, and Professional Development; A Short Introduction and Bibliography, available at www.ee.ucl.ac.uk/~mflanaga/thresholds .html. See the Framework Wordpress site for current news and resources.

ACRL Information Literacy Competency Standards Review Task Force. "Task Force Recommendations." ACRL AC12 Doc 13.1, June 2, 2012. www.ala.org/acrl/ sites/ala.org.acrl/files/content/standards/ils_recomm.pdf.

American Association for School Librarians. *Standards for the 21st-Century Learner*. Chicago: American Library Association, 2007. www.ala.org/aasl/sites/ ala.org.aasl/files/content/guidelinesandstandards/learningstandards/AASL_ LearningStandards.pdf.

Blackmore, Margaret. "Student Engagement with Information: Applying a Threshold Concept Approach to Information Literacy Development." Paper presented at the 3rd Biennial Threshold Concepts Symposium: Exploring Transformative Dimensions of Threshold Concepts, Sydney, Australia, July 1–2, 2010.

Carmichael, Patrick. "Tribes, Territories, and Threshold Concepts: Educational Materialisms at Work in Higher Education." *Educational Philosophy and Theory* 44, no. S1 (2012): 31–42.

Coonan, Emma. *A New Curriculum for Information Literacy: Teaching Learning; Perceptions of Information Literacy*. Arcadia Project, Cambridge University Library, July 2011. http://ccfil.pbworks.com/f/emma_report_final.pdf.

Cousin, Glynis. "An Introduction to Threshold Concepts." *Planet* 17 (December 2006): 4–5.

———. "Threshold Concepts, Troublesome Knowledge and Emotional Capital: An Exploration into Learning about Others." In *Overcoming Barriers to Student Understanding: Threshold Concepts and Troublesome Knowledge*, edited by Jan H. F. Meyer and Ray Land, 134–47. London and New York: Routledge, 2006.

Gibson, Craig, and Trudi Jacobson. "Informing and Extending the Draft ACRL Information Literacy Framework for Higher Education: An Overview and Avenues for Research." *College and Research Libraries* 75, no. 3 (May 2014): 250–4.

Head, Alison J. "Project Information Literacy: What Can Be Learned about the Information-Seeking Behavior of Today's College Students?" Paper presented at the ACRL National Conference, Indianapolis, IN, April 10–13, 2013.

Hofer, Amy R., Lori Townsend, and Korey Brunetti. "Troublesome Concepts and Information Literacy: Investigating Threshold Concepts for IL Instruction." *portal: Libraries and the Academy* 12, no. 4 (2012): 387–405.

Jacobson, Trudi E., and Thomas P. Mackey. "Proposing a Metaliteracy Model to Redefine Information Literacy." *Communications in Information Literacy* 7, no. 2 (2013): 84–91.

Kuhlthau, Carol C. "Rethinking the 2000 ACRL Standards: Some Things to Consider." *Communications in Information Literacy* 7, no. 3 (2013): 92–7.

———. *Seeking Meaning: A Process Approach to Library and Information Services.* Westport, CT: Libraries Unlimited, 2004.

Limberg, Louise, Mikael Alexandersson, Annika Lantz-Andersson, and Lena Folkesson. "What Matters? Shaping Meaningful Learning through Teaching Information Literacy." *Libri* 58, no. 2 (2008): 82–91.

Lloyd, Annemaree. *Information Literacy Landscapes: Information Literacy in Education, Workplace and Everyday Contexts.* Oxford: Chandos Publishing, 2010.

Lupton, Mandy Jean. *The Learning Connection: Information Literacy and the Student Experience.* Blackwood, South Australia: Auslib Press, 2004.

Mackey, Thomas P., and Trudi E. Jacobson. *Metaliteracy: Reinventing Information Literacy to Empower Learners.* Chicago: Neal-Schuman, 2014.

Martin, Justine. "Refreshing Information Literacy." *Communications in Information Literacy* 7, no. 2 (2013): 114–27.

Meyer, Jan, and Ray Land. *Threshold Concepts and Troublesome Knowledge: Linkages to Ways of Thinking and Practicing within the Disciplines.* Edinburgh, UK: University of Edinburgh, 2003.

Meyer, Jan H. F., Ray Land, and Caroline Baillie. "Editors' Preface." In *Threshold Concepts and Transformational Learning*, edited by Jan H. F. Meyer, Ray Land, and Caroline Baillie, ix–xlii. Rotterdam, Netherlands: Sense Publishers, 2010.

Middendorf, Joan, and David Pace. "Decoding the Disciplines: A Model for Helping Students Learn Disciplinary Ways of Thinking." *New Directions for Teaching and Learning*, no. 98 (2004): 1–12.

Oakleaf, Megan. "A Roadmap for Assessing Student Learning Using the New Framework for Information Literacy for Higher Education." *Journal of Academic Librarianship* 40, no. 5 (September 2014): 510–4.

Secker, Jane. *A New Curriculum for Information Literacy: Expert Consultation Report.* Arcadia Project, Cambridge University Library, July 2011. http://ccfil.pbworks .com/f/Expert_report_final.pdf.

Townsend, Lori, Korey Brunetti, and Amy R. Hofer. "Threshold Concepts and Information Literacy." *portal: Libraries and the Academy* 11, no. 3 (2011): 853–69.

Tucker, Virginia, Christine Bruce, Sylvia Edwards, and Judith Weedman. "Learning Portals: Analyzing Threshold Concept Theory for LIS Education." *Journal of Education for Library and Information Science* 55, no. 2 (2014): 150–65.

Wiggins, Grant, and Jay McTighe. *Understanding by Design.* Alexandria, VA: Association for Supervision and Curriculum Development, 2004.

Bibliography

ACRL. *Framework for Information Literacy for Higher Education*. Chicago: American Library Association, 2015. www.ala.org/acrl/standards/ilframework.

ACRL. *Information Literacy Competency Standards for Higher Education*. Chicago: American Library Association, 2000. www.ala.org/acrl/standards/informationliteracy competency.

Alexander, Patricia A., Jonna M. Kulikowich, and Sharon K. Schulze. "How Subject-Matter Knowledge Affects Recall and Interest." *American Educational Research Journal* 31, no. 2 (Summer 1994): 313–37.

Alonso-Alonso, Miguel. "Cocoa Flavanols and Cognition: Regaining Chocolate in Old Age?" *American Journal of Clinical Nutrition* 101 (2015): 423–24.

Argyris, Chris. "Teaching Smart People How to Learn." *Harvard Business Review* 69, no. 3 (1991): 99–109.

Badke, William. "Content, Content Everywhere" *Online Magazine* 34, no. 2 (March 2010): 52–54. www.onlinemag.net.

Bain, Ken. *What the Best College Students Do*. Cambridge, MA: Belknap Press of Harvard University, 2012.

Barnett, Susan M., and Stephen J. Ceci. "When and Where Do We Apply What We Learn? A Taxonomy for Far Transfer." *Psychological Bulletin* 128, no. 4 (2002): 612–37.

Barradell, Sarah. "The Identification of Threshold Concepts: A Review of Theoretical Complexities and Methodological Challenges." *Higher Education* 65 (2013): 265–76.

Belander, Jackie, Ning Zou, Jenny Rushing Mills, Claire Holmes, and Megan Oakleaf. "Project RAILS: Lessons Learned about Rubric Assessment of Information Literacy Skills." *portal: Libraries and the Academy* 15, no. 4 (2015): 623–44.

Belenky, Daniel M., and Timothy J. Nokes-Malach. "Mastery-Approach Goals and Knowledge Transfer: An Investigation into the Effects of Task Structure and Framing Instructions." *Learning and Individual Differences* 25 (2013): 21–34.

Berg, Jacob. "Scholarship as Conversation: The Response to the Framework for Information Literacy." *ACRLog* (blog), January 21, 2015. http://acrlog.org/2015/01/21/scholarship-as-conversation-the-response-to-the-framework-for-information-literacy.

Billing, David. "Teaching for Transfer of Core/Key Skills in Higher Education: Cognitive Skills." *Higher Education* 53 (2007): 483–516.

Bishop, Michaelle, and Brandon West. "Using Primary Sources to Help Students Discover Their Voices in the Research Process." *LOEX Quarterly* 41 (2015): 2–3, 10.

Bondy, Elizabeth, Elyse Hambacher, Amy S. Murphy, Rachel Wolkenhauer, and Desi Krell. "Developing Critical Social Justice Literacy in an Online Seminar." *Equity and Excellence in Education* 48, no. 2 (2015): 227–48.

Brookfield, Stephen D. *Teaching for Critical Thinking: Tools and Techniques to Help Students Question Their Assumptions*. San Francisco: Jossey-Bass, 2012.

Brown, Peter C., Henry L. Roediger III, and Mark A. McDaniel. *Make It Stick: The Science of Successful Learning*. Cambridge, MA: Belknap Press of Harvard University Press, 2014.

Buchanan, Heidi E., and Beth A. McDonough. *One-Shot Library Instruction Survival Guide*. Chicago: ALA Editions, 2014.

Burkhardt, Andy. "Threshold Concepts in Practice: An Example from the Classroom." *Information Tyrannosaur*, March 4, 2014. http://andyburkhardt.com/2014/03/04/threshold-concepts-in-practice-an-example-from-the-classroom.

Campbell, Lisa, Diana Matthews, and Nance Lempinen-Leedy. "Wake Up Information Literacy Instruction: Ideas for Student Engagement." *Journal of Library Administration* 55, no. 7 (2015): 577–86.

Casale, Michael B., Jessica L. Roeder, and F. Gregory Ashby. "Analogical Transfer in Perceptual Categorization." *Memory and Cognition* 40 (2012): 434–49.

Chen, Zhe, Lei Mo, and Ryan Honomichi. "Having the Memory of an Elephant: Long-Term Retrieval and the Use of Analogues in Problem Solving." *Journal of Experimental Psychology: General* 133, no. 3 (September 2004): 415–33.

Cheuk, Bonnie. "Delivering Business Value through Information Literacy in the Workplace." *Libri* 58 (2008): 137–43.

Clifford, Margaret M. "Students Need Challenge, Not Easy Success." *Educational Leadership* 48, no. 1 (September 1990): 22–26.

Crawford, Gregory. "The Academic Library and Student Retention and Graduation: An Exploratory Study." *portal: Libraries and the Academy* 15, no. 1 (January 2015): 41–57.

Critical Thinking Community. "An Overview of How to Design Instruction Using Critical Thinking Concepts." www.criticalthinking.org/pages/an-overview-of-how-to-design-instruction-using-critical-thin/439.

———. "Critical Thinking, Moral Integrity and Citizenship." www.criticalthinking.org/pages/critical_thinking_moral_integrity_and_citizenship_teaching_for_the_intellectual_virtues/487.

Eberhard, Jessica Masari, Sam Corbett, and Susan Gail Taylor. "Analyzing Ads: Race." WritingCommons.http://writingcommons.org/index.php/open-text/information-literacy/visual-literacy/ad-analysis/437-analyzing-ads-race.

Eckersley, Peter. "How Online Tracking Companies Know Most of What You Do Online (and What Social Networks Are Doing to Help Them)." Electronic Frontier Foundation, September 21, 2009. https://www.eff.org/deeplinks/2009/09/online-trackers-and-social-networks.

Ericsson, K. Anders, Ralf Th. Krampe, and Clemens Tesch-Romer. "The Role of Deliberate Practice in the Acquisition of Expert Performance." *Psychological Review* 100, no. 3 (1993): 363–406.

Feldman, Susan. "The High Cost of Not Finding Information." *KM World* 13, no. 3 (March 2004): 8–10.

Ferran-Ferrer, Nuria, Julia Minguillon, and Mario Perez-Montoro. "Key Factors in the Transfer of Information-Related Competencies between Academic, Workplace and Daily Life Contexts." *Journal of the American Society for Information Sciences and Technology* 64, no. 6 (2013): 1112–21.

Forshaw, Mark. *Critical Thinking for Psychology: A Student Guide.* Hoboken, NJ: Wiley Blackwell, 2012.

Freeley, Austin J., and David L. Steinberg. *Argumentation and Debate.* 10th ed. Australia: Wadsworth, 2000.

Gentner, Dedre, Jeffrey Loewenstein, and Leigh Thompson. "Learning and Transfer: A General Role for Analogical Encoding." *Journal of Educational Psychology* 95, no. 2 (June 2003): 393–408.

Grady, Denise. "Medical Journal Cites Misleading Drug Research." *New York Times,* November 10, 1999. www.nytimes.com/1999/11/10/us/medical-journal-cites-misleading-drug-research.html.

Gwyer, Roisin. "Identifying and Exploring Future Trends Impacting on Academic Libraries: A Mixed Methodology Using Journal Content Analysis, Focus Groups and Trend Reports." *New Review of Academic Librarianship* 21, no. 3 (September–December 2015): 1–17.

Hofer, Amy R., Lori Townsend, and Korey Brunetti. "Troublesome Concepts and Information Literacy: Investigating Threshold Concepts for IL Instruction." *portal: Libraries and the Academy* 12, no. 4 (October 2012): 387–405.

Holyoak, Keith J., and Paul Thagard. *Mental Leaps: Analogy in Creative Thought.* Cambridge, MA: MIT Press, 1995.

Huff, Darrell. *How to Lie with Statistics*. New York: Norton, 1954.

Kahneman, Daniel. *Thinking Fast and Slow*. New York: Farrar, Straus and Giroux, 2011.

Kalmansohn, David. "Turmeric/Curcumin." *Vegetarian Times,* October 2015. www.press reader.com/usa/vegetarian-times/20151001/281728383283057/TextView.

Kaplowitz, Joan. *Designing Information Literacy Instruction: The Teaching Tripod Approach*. Lanham, MD: Rowman and Littlefield, 2014.

Klipfel, Kevin Michael. "This I Overheard . . . Threshold Concepts Getting Laughed Out of the Room." *Rule Number One: A Library Blog,* November 3, 2014. http://rule numberoneblog.com/2014/11/03/this-i-overheard-threshold-concepts-getting -laughed-out-of-the-room.

Krishnamurthy, Balachander, and Craig E. Wills. "On the Leakage of Personally Identifiable Information via Online Social Networks." *WOSN '09,* Proceedings of the 2nd ACM Workshop on Online Social Networks, Barcelona, Spain, August 17, 2009.

Kuglitsch, Rebecca Z. "Teaching for Transfer: Reconciling the Framework with Disciplinary Information Literacy." *portal: Libraries and the Academy* 15, no. 3 (July 2015): 457–70.

Jacobs, Heidi L. M. "Posing the Wikipedia 'Problem': Information Literacy and the Praxis of Problem-Posing in Library Instruction." In *Critical Library Instruction: Theories and Methods,* edited by Maria T. Accardi, Emily Drabinski, and Alana Kumbien. Duluth: Library Juice Press, 2009.

LaFrance, Adrienne. "Raiders of the Lost Web." *The Atlantic,* October 14, 2015. www .theatlantic.com/technology/archive/2015/10/raiders-of-the-lost-web/409210.

Land, R., and J. H. F. Meyer. "Threshold Concepts and Troublesome Knowledge: An Introduction." In *Overcoming Barriers to Student Understanding: Threshold Concepts and Troublesome Knowledge,* edited by J. H. F. Meyer and R. Land, 19–32. London: Routledge, 2006.

Land, R., J. H. F. Meyer, and C. Baillie. "Editor's Preface." In *Threshold Concepts and Transformational Learning,* edited by J. H. F. Meyer, R. Land, and C. Baillie, ix-xliii. Rotterdam: Sense Publishers, 2010.

Lloyd, Annemaree. "Working Information." *Journal of Workplace Learning* 18, no. 3 (2006): 186–98.

Mackey, Thomas, and Trudy Jacobson. *Metaliteracy: Reinventing Information Literacy to Empower Learners*. Chicago: ALA Neal-Schuman, 2014.

Massee, Laura A., Karin Ried, Matthew Pase, Nikolaj Travica, Jaesshanth Yoganathan, Andrew Scholey, Helen Macpherson, Greg Kennedy, Avni Sali, and Andrew Pipingas. "The Acute and Sub-Chronic Effects of Cocoa Flavanols on Mood, Cognitive and Cardiovascular Health in Young Healthy Adults: A Randomized Controlled Trial." *Frontiers in Pharmacology* 6, no. 93 (May 2015): 1–14.

Mastroiacovo, Daniela, Catherine Kwik-Uribe, Davide Grassi, Stefano Necozione, Angelo Raffaele, Luana Pistacchio, Roberta Righetti et al. "Cocoa Flavanol Consumption Improves Cognitive Function, Blood Pressure Control, and Metabolic

Profile in Elderly Subjects: The Cocoa, Cognition, and Aging (CoCoA) Study—A Randomized Controlled Trial." *American Journal of Clinical Nutrition* 101 (2015): 538–48.

Meyer, Jan, and Ray Land. "Threshold Concepts and Troublesome Knowledge: Linkages to Ways of Thinking and Practicing within the Disciplines." ETL Project, Occasional Report 4. Edinburgh: University of Edinburgh, 2003.

Morgan, Patrick K. "Foundational Assumptions in Threshold Concepts and Information Literacy." Association of College and Research Libraries Conference, Portland, OR, March 25–28, 2015. www.ala.org/acrl/sites/ala.org.acrl/files/content/conferences/confsandpreconfs/2015/Morgan.pdf.

Moore, Jessie L. "Designing for Transfer: A Threshold Concept." *Journal of Faculty Development* 26, no. 3 (September 2012): 19–24.

Mulcahy, Monica Dianne. "Turning Around the Question of 'Transfer' in Education: Tracing the Sociomaterial." *Educational Philosophy and Theory* 45, no. 12 (2013): 1276–89.

"The Murky World of Third Party Web Tracking." *MIT Technology Review*, September 12, 2014. www.technologyreview.com/view/530741/the-murky-world-of-third-party-web-tracking.

Murley, Diane. "Innovative Instructional Methods." *Legal Reference Services Quarterly* 6, no. 1–2 (2007): 171–85.

Oakleaf, Megan. "A Roadmap for Assessing Student Learning Using the New Framework for Information Literacy for Higher Education." http://meganoakleaf.info/framework.pdf.

O'Sullivan, Carmel. "Is Information Literacy Relevant in the Real World?" *References Services Review* 30, no. 1 (2002): 7–14.

Pack, Jenna. "Breaking Down an Image." Writing Commons Open Text. http://writingcommons.org/index.php/open-text/information-literacy/visual-literacy/breaking-down-an-image.

Palfrey, John. *Biblio Tech: Why Libraries Are More Important Than Ever in the Age of Google*. New York: Basic Books, 2015.

Pandey, Anshul Vikram, Katharina Rall, Margaret L. Satterthwaite, Oded Nov, and Enrico Bertini. "How Deceptive Are Deceptive Visualizations? An Empirical Analysis of Common Distortion Techniques." *CHI 2015*, April 18–23, 2015. Seoul, Republic of Korea. http://faculty.poly.edu/~onov/Pandey_et_al_CHI_2015.pdf.

Parikh, Ravi. "How to Lie with Data Visualization." *Heap Data Blog*, April 14, 2014. http://data.heapanalytics.com/how-to-lie-with-data-visualization.

Peddada, Krishi V., Kranti Venkata Peddada, Surendra K. Shukla, Anusha Mishra, and Vivek Verma. "Role of Curcumin in Common Musculoskeletal Disorders: A Review of Current Laboratory, Translational and Clinical Data." *Orthopaedic Surgery* 7 (2015): 222–31.

Perkins, D. M., and Gavriel Salomon. "Teaching for Transfer." *Educational Leadership* 46, no. 1 (September 1988): 22–32.

Quinn, Todd, and Lora Leligdon. "Executive MBA Students' Information Skills and Knowledge: Discovering the Difference between Work and Academics." *Journal of Business and Finance Librarianship* 19 (2014): 234–55.

Rennie, Drummond. "Fair Conduct and Fair Reporting of Clinical Trials." *JAMA* 282, no. 18 (November 10, 1999): 1766–68.

Rohrer, Doug, and Harold Pashler. "Increasing Retention without Increasing Study Time." *Current Directions in Psychological Science* 16, no. 4 (August 2007): 183–86.

Seeber, Kevin Patrick. "Teaching 'Format as a Process' in an Era of Web-Scale Discovery." *Reference Services Review* 43, no. 1 (2015): 19–30.

"Should You Work Chocolate into Your Diet?" *Harvard Health Letter*, June 2015. www .health.harvard.edu/newsletters/harvard_health_letter.

Simon, Herbert A., and William G. Chase. "Skill in Chess: Experiments with Chess-Playing Tasks and Computer Simulation of Skilled Performance Throw Light on Some Human Perceptual and Memory Processes." *American Scientist* 61, no. 4 (July–August 1973): 394–403.

Sokolof, Jason. "Information Literacy in the Workplace: Employer Expectations." *Journal of Business and Finance Librarianship*, 17, no. 1 (2012): 1–17.

Townsend, Lori, Korey Brunetti, and Amy R. Hofer. "Threshold Concepts and Information Literacy." *portal: Libraries and the Academy* 11, no. 3 (July 2011): 853–69.

Weiner, Sharon. "Information Literacy and the Workforce: A Review." *Education Libraries* 34, no. 2 (Winter 2011): 7–4.

Wilkinson, Lane. "The Problem with Threshold Concepts." *Sense and Reference: A Philosophical Library Blog*, June 19, 2014. https://senseandreference.wordpress.com.

———. "Is Authority Constructed and Contextual?" *Sense and Reference: A Philosophical Library Blog*, June 15, 2014. https://senseandreference.wordpress.com.

———. "Is Scholarship a Conversation?" *Sense and Reference: A Philosophical Library Blog*, July 10, 2014. https://senseandreference.wordpress.com.

———. "Does Information Have Value?" *Sense and Reference: A Philosophical Library Blog*, August 5, 2014. https://senseandreference.wordpress.com.

———. "Is Searching Exploration?" *Sense and Reference: A Philosophical Library Blog*, July 29, 2014. https://senseandreference.wordpress.com.

———. "Is Research Inquiry?" *Sense and Reference: A Philosophical Library Blog*, July 15, 2014. https://senseandreference.wordpress.com.

Willingham, Daniel T. *Why Don't Students Like School?* San Francisco: Jossey-Bass, 2009.

Wilson, Patrick. *Second-Hand Knowledge: An Inquiry into Cognitive Authority*. Westport, CT: Greenwood, 1983.

Index